The

Theater
Director's
Primer

GARY P. COHEN

HEINEMANN
Portsmouth, NH

Heinemann
A division of Reed Elsevier Inc.
361 Hanover Street
Portsmouth, NH 03801–3912
www.heinemanndrama.com

Offices and agents throughout the world

Library of Congress Cataloging-in-Publication Data
Cohen, Gary P. (Gary Philip), 1952–
    The theater director's primer / Gary P. Cohen.
        p. cm.
    ISBN 0-325-00727-6 (alk. paper)
    1. Theater—Production and direction.   I. Title.
PN2053.C57 2005
792.02'33—dc22   2005003920

Editor: Lisa A. Barnett
Production: Vicki Kasabian
Cover design: Night & Day Design
Typesetter: Monotype
Manufacturing: Louise Richardson

Printed in the United States of America on acid-free paper
09 08 07 06 05   DA   1 2 3 4 5

Contents

Contents

Acknowledgments

I would like to thank Michelle Massa and Holly Logue, both excellent directors, for their input into this book. They kept me on track, focused, and on my toes.

I would also like to thank John Prignano, senior vice president at Music Theatre International, for clarifying several points regarding licensing agreements and the law.

A warm thank-you to Lisa Barnett, my editor at Heinemann, for her constant encouragement and wonderful sense of humor.

Special thanks to all my director, designer, and actor friends for their answers to my e-mail queries, and to composer Mark Baron for his thoughts on sequencing and orchestrations.

Last, a thank-you to my parents, who introduced me to the original cast album of *The Music Man* when I was just a kid, and have always supported my decision to work in theater.

Preface

According to *The Oxford Universal Dictionary,* a director is: *one who or that which directs, rules or guides; a guide; a conductor; a superintendent.* While this is indeed true, it is dramatically lacking in defining what a stage director actually is and does. In my experience, a director is the artistic head of a theatrical production, but might also be called upon to be:

- an artist who can take the written word and transform it into a living, breathing entity that is cleverly staged, well paced, and full of fascinating performances;
- a translator who elicits from the dialogue an understanding that guides the actors through a performance and that can communicate the author's meaning and intention;
- an actor who, on occasion, can perform in order to demonstrate his ideas to the actual actors;
- an associate scenic, lighting, and costume designer who needs a working knowledge of each discipline in order to make sure his or her concepts are sound and to then convey these concepts to the primary designers;
- a politician who carefully interacts with one or more producers and/or a board of directors, knowing when to be proprietary to his vision while working within the house rules;
- a financial wizard who can often make a silk purse out of a sow's ear by creating a wonderful production that stays within the budget;
- a psychologist who, when necessary, can gently soothe the psyches of those artists on his project; and
- an historian who spends a great deal of time analyzing and researching all aspects of a show and its history via books, films, and the Internet.

Does a director really need to be proficient at all these tasks? Possibly not. But I'd be willing to wager that if you have ever directed a play or musical you most likely have found yourself touching on many of these points, even if unwittingly.

Think back. How often did you turn to an actor and instruct, "No, say it like this . . ." or "put the emphasis here"? Well, you were an actor for a moment, however fleeting. Did you ever explain to the lighting designer that you need the scene to feel a bit colder or tell the set designer that the door needs to open out rather than in? Maybe you told the costumer that the day dress appears a bit too contemporary. If you did, you were reacting like a designer. Were you ever in a meeting discussing the budget with the board of directors, and they told you the two-story set design was going to be just too expensive? But, you protested, if some of the existing flats you saw in storage were properly adapted and refinished, they would do the trick. Maybe it was suggested to you that a producer's niece would be just perfect for a role and you had to tactfully suggest that you saw the character differently, however, there was this other role . . . That's being a politician . . . and one who has done his or her homework.

How did you handle the temperamental ensemble members when they felt their time was underutilized during the rehearsal? Diplomatically, I hope, because it often happens. And when the costumer asked if the skirts should be knee length, calf length, or ankle length, did you know the answer because just last evening you watched a documentary on the time period?

It takes a unique mind-set and personality to juggle all of these positions and to do it well. And it sure helps to be well prepared. A great many directors are content to "specialize" in what is often referred to as an "actor's director"—devoting 90 percent of their time to performances and leaving technical values solely to the designers. This is acceptable, and there is no doubt that the actors require the guidance of a director foremost. But I'm not truly comfortable unless I have input into all the disciplines that go into creating a stage production.

For me, acting, costuming, lighting, set designing, props, and, if applicable, choreography and music direction are all parts of the directorial puzzle—and all the pieces must fit together properly for the design to look right.

What separates the professionals from the amateurs is not money, but attention to details. You need to make sure that every aspect of the show is complete, down to the most minute detail, and that all elements fit into the big picture. That is the key to a successful show.

My personal philosophy is that the same high standards and disciplines should apply in every venue. There is nothing more satisfying than to see a group of high school students rise to the level of professionalism found in a regional theater. If you are directing on a community level, it is quite rewarding to know in your heart of hearts that your show rivals what you've seen on a national tour or at a regional venue. The responsibility to encourage every group to rise to the highest levels possible belongs to the director. From preproduction to the very first rehearsal to opening night, the director sets the standards.

Once a director has a clear understanding of his or her role, then regardless of whether the production is mounted in two weeks under Equity rules and regulations, in a New York rehearsal studio or you take six weeks of evenings and weekends in a converted barn, a satisfying and creative theatrical experience can be had.

For directors just starting out: I hope this book will help you avoid some pitfalls and encourage you to do your homework and to refine your communication skills. For working directors: this book might provide you with some new insights and a refresher course in the art. If you are working on Broadway, return this book and get your money back—you can teach me some things!

I invite any reader of this book to email me with questions, thoughts, arguments, or insights at www.pipoffice@playsinthepark .com. The content of this book is volatile and subject to varying opinions; I welcome yours.

Getting the Job

Okay, you've put your hand on a rock, looked up to the heavens and shouted, "I'm a director!" Now what?

Well, you've probably got more experience, expertise, and credits than that, but nonetheless, how do you go about letting theaters know that you're the right person for the job? That you have what it takes to direct their show? Competition is fierce in many areas of the country—especially for paying gigs, so presenting your best image is crucial.

In New Jersey, where I reside and work, there is a profusion of theaters. On every level—Equity, college, community, and high school—one merely has to travel a few miles—in some cases a few blocks—to find live entertainment. One town where I have worked on the high school and community-theater levels boasts no less than six theatrical venues. There is a community theater that has been around nearly a century. There is a repertory company that uses scores of young people in each show and changes its home yearly from the high school to the churches and the temples. There is a professional Equity theater-in-residence at the local community college. The high school does a straight play in the autumn and a musical in the spring; and two to three of the middle schools do one or two productions each year.

While this may seem like theatrical heaven, there is, unfortunately, only a limited actor base from which to cast, and each theater struggles to recruit designers and backstage staff. If the theater seeks volunteer designers or pays just a small stipend, staffing a show becomes all the more difficult, and many theaters cannot afford to pay for any of their talent—on either side of the curtain.

A good director might therefore be in demand and can many times be choosy about which theaters to work at and which shows to do. Unfortunately, this type of situation often encourages less-than-stellar directors to ingratiate themselves into theaters where they can get in over their heads.

New Jersey (and other heavily populated metropolitan areas), however, may be the exception. I recently had the privilege of being the keynote speaker at a conference of community theaters in Pennsylvania, and during the Q & A section of my talk I learned that the exact opposite was true in many areas of the country. I was told that the farther you get from New York, the fewer theaters there are. In one rural area of Pennsylvania there is only one community theater for miles, and the only LORT[1] venue is twenty minutes away. They felt that there was a dearth of directors, and one of the questions many asked me is "how do we find good directors"? Many of these theater groups were concerned that only two or three directors helmed every show, season after season, which tended to make for stale productions and cliquish casts.

Depending on where you live and the abundance or lack of theaters within your area, you will still need to sell yourself to board members, producers, and artistic directors. Unless you are lucky enough to manage your own theater or have no competition from other directors, you will have to convince people that you can handle the daunting challenge of directing a play or musical.

Plenty of directors are not confined to one geographical area. They spend their lives traveling from city to city and theater to theater, building their resumes and gaining experience. These "career" directors harbor hopes that a national tour or a Broadway show will eventually come their way. They know that traveling from city to city doing community theater won't lead to a Broadway gig, but they are gathering experience that could lead to a professional regional theater job, which might then lead elsewhere.

Even if you're not directing on Broadway, and assuming you have a few shows under your belt, a resume is in order. Without overstating the obvious, a resume should be clean, concise, and professional-looking. Using a computer with spell check makes that

---

1 LORT refers to the League of Regional Theaters, a professional Equity organization. For more information, visit: www.lort.org/.

Figure 1–1 is a fictitious resume as an example:

Lester Bart
(SSDC eligible)
23 North Broad Street
West Highland, KY 08743
Home phone: 543-879-0934
Cell phone: 543-655-2218
Fax machine: 543-987-2273
Email: LBart@hotmail.com

Education
BFA in Directing, Kean University, Union, NJ 19980

Experience (Professional/Equity)

Drama/Comedy

Sylvia	Lions Gate Regional Theater Portsmouth, Virginia LORT C Theater
American Buffalo	Lions Gate Regional Theater

Musicals

Hello, Dolly!	Forum Theater Group Fairfield, Connecticut LORT C Theater
Sweet Charity	Forum Theater Group

Experience (Nonprofessional/College/Community)

Drama/Comedy

You Can't Take It with You	Archbrook Community Theater Newton, Massachusetts
As You Like It	Shakespeare in the Park Portsmouth, Virginia
Mamet One-Acts	Brookdale College Westlake, Virginia

Musicals

Cabaret	Hempstead Players Hempstead, New York
The Fantasticks	Hempstead Players

---

very easy. The resumes should give readers all the information they might need to contact you and to see at a glance the kind of work experience you have had. Unlike an actor's resume, I would leave off the special skills, simply because you will list them in the cover letter that will accompany your resume.

Note the reference to SSDC under Lester's name. This is an independent national labor union called the Society of Stage Directors and Choreographers, similar to Actor's Equity for performers. Their website contains all the information you need to find out what they do and how to become a member, which is what you will want to do if you are seeking a professional career as a director. You can find them at www.ssdc.org.

The sample resume divides experience into professional and nonprofessional categories (professional defined by the theater's status, not the quality of the work) and then further categorizes the musicals and nonmusicals. This is merely one way to do it. If you have no "professional" credits you might merely divide the comedies and dramas from the musicals. If you don't do musicals, find some other way to list your credits. As long as it is clean and concise, it'll work.

If you are mailing your resume to various theaters, you'll want to include a cover letter. In an interview you will have the opportunity to go into further detail. The resume and cover letter should highlight the experiences and skills you possess that are relevant to each particular position.

Here's an invented cover letter as an example:

To Whom It May Concern (or Dear Artistic Director or, ideally, a specific person's name):

By way of an introduction, my name is Lester Bart and I am applying for a directing position at your theater.

I have had extensive experience directing both musicals and nonmusicals on many levels since my graduation with a BFA in Directing from Kean University.

My experience has taken me from the college level to community theaters to professional assignments at two LORT C Regional Theaters. I am currently SSDC-eligible.

I feel that I am a very organized director who uses the actors' time wisely. I have worked successfully in summer stock situations under pressure. I thoroughly research each show and thus work well with the various designers. Because I have also occasionally designed sets and lights, I am conversant with the language needed to communicate with the design staff. I also respect the budget restraints of each theater and can work within them. Most of all, I feel I have excellent people skills, a trait I feel necessary in such a collaborative discipline as theater.

Attached are references from many of the producers I have worked with. Feel free to call them for further information. I have also attached copies of some of the reviews I have received for my work.

I look forward to the opportunity of an interview and your positive response to this letter.

Yours truly,
Lester Bart

Of course, this example uses my style and language; please don't copy it word for word, especially if that's not the way you write or talk. But you get the idea.

If your resume is quite lengthy, you might want to eliminate some of the least recent or least significant credits to create a shortened version, with a note on the bottom telling interested parties that additional information is available upon request or, with technology affording us a variety of ways of sharing information, that they might further research your experience on the Internet. A close friend of mine, David Christopher, has created a quite lengthy Web page devoted to both his directing and his acting experience, being careful to separate the two. While I firmly believe that a director who has acted can bring special insight into his handling of actors, you wouldn't want to crowd and confuse a resume with both credits. David has given permission for readers of this book to access his site, which can be found at: www.arcadianclock.com/dru/resume.

Support materials are also important in selling yourself and your work. Certainly, attaching some color photos of your productions would be a good idea. Luckily we don't have to spend a fortune having prints made at camera stores any longer (although if you can afford it, professional glossy prints are still the best) because you can create effective photos using a digital camera, a good printer, and high-quality paper at home or a local Kinko's. Including a photo or two of a dramatic moment from a straight play or a well-composed ensemble scene from a musical can show off your skills—a picture being worth a thousand words, of course.

A demo video might also be a good way to show off, *but*, this is a gray area legally. Although videotaping an entire production is against your licensing agreement with the companies that grant permission to do the plays and musicals and, in the case of a professional show, against Equity rules, you might inquire if a small excerpt—less than two minutes, say—would be allowed. Sometimes you can get permission for archival footage, footage used for securing grants, or for other promotions. Before videotaping, secure permission from the theater, the licensing company (Samuel French, Music Theater International, etc.), and the performers. If you can secure permission, it's worth doing, because including a VHS tape or even a DVD gives the potential employers a firsthand opportunity to see your work.

If you currently have a show on the boards or an up-and-coming production in the same general area as the theater where you are seeking employment, then by all means invite the producers/board of directors to see your work. Arrange for tickets—even transportation if you really want to make an impression—and double-check that everything is perfect. Make sure the tickets are indeed at the box office, that they are comps or paid for by you, that they are good seats, and that you got the right time and date.

If you are successful in luring your potential employer to see your show, consider carefully whether you wish to seek them out afterward. You don't want to make it awkward for them, in case there were elements that they didn't like—elements beyond your control, of course. Following up with a phone call a day or two later might be the best route to follow.

Personal recommendations from other theaters are very important. If you had a good experience at a theater, there is nothing wrong with asking the producer or a member of the board to write a generic letter for your portfolio. If they write it right after the show closes, chances are it will glow more than if you ask for a recommendation months or years later. Grab them while they're still high on audience reaction and great reviews.

What are theaters looking for when they seek out new directors? Knowing the answer to this question will help you address their concerns. A producer—and when I refer to the "producer" it is shorthand for the producing organization, whether it is an individual producer, an artistic director, a production manager, the theater president, a whole board of directors, or any other variation or committee—will want to know about your personality as well as your talent. When I seek out a new director for my theater in New Jersey (Plays-in-the-Park, www.playsinthepark.com), I look for a number of criteria, not all of which apply in every situation:

- What other theaters have hired this director—are they theaters that resemble in any way the scope or mission statement of my theater?
- Does the director's resume indicate experience with productions that relate in some way to the show I'm producing—a big musical, for example, or something Shakespearean if I'm doing *Twelfth Night*?
- Can the director work within my budget?
- Can the director relate and communicate with the scenic, costume, and lighting designers, the choreographer, and the musical director?
- Can the director relate and communicate with me, the producer?
- Can the director work well with actors, communicating his or her ideas pleasantly to them?
- Are there other producers I can contact to get answers to some of my questions—to get a personal recommendation?
- Can I see an example of the director's work—either via appropriate production photos, videotape, or a current performance?
- Can I contact any actors whose opinion I trust and who have worked with this director before?
- Will this director work within the mission statement of my theater? Can he or she re-create the flavor of the original production if that's what is required, or can he or she come up with an inventive new approach to the property, if that's what I am seeking?

In Chapter 4 I discuss in detail a director's approach to a particular show—whether the director will try to re-create as closely as possible the original production given the resources available, or whether the director will reimagine it, setting it in another locale or time; cast it in a dramatically different way (such as cross-gender, or color blind); or change it in some other fashion. But for the purposes of getting a job, it is helpful for the director to know which option the producer is looking for. Having this information will go a long way to making the interview the best it can be.

I Got an Interview!! Now What?

Armed with a distinctive and impressive resume and an effective cover letter, chances are good you'll get an interview. The interview can often make the difference in your getting the job. While your resume made the very first impression, the impact you have in person can make or break the deal. Remain true to who you are, present yourself in the best possible light, and never intentionally fabricate your experience.

While presenting yourself in the best possible light doesn't mean dressing in an Armani suit, it does mean that you should dress professionally. Presenting the image of an avant-garde director straight from the Performance Garage might have worked in the sixties, but probably would be disconcerting outside of Greenwich Village nowadays.

You should also be well prepared. Know the show(s) the theater is doing. If at all possible, know the theater space itself prior to the meeting. Many years ago I went to an interview at a theater that was looking for a director to stage *Best Little Whorehouse in Texas,* a play I had never directed, in a theater I had been to only once. The interview went very well when I talked about my experience, my working methods with actors and crew, and my knowledge of set and lighting design. But when I was asked, "So how would you adapt this show to our space" I was caught off guard and it showed. I did not get the job. After that interview I was always ready for such a question.

Sing your praises at the interview, but do it in such a way that you don't seem overly egotistical. Talk about your method of working, but make sure you also appear adaptable to methods that their theater has found workable in the past. Be flexible; be adaptable. At my theater, Plays-in-the-Park, we have a very set way of auditioning—one that has worked for forty-two years as of this writing—but it is definitely tailored to this particular venue. When working at another theater I have to be prepared to work within their systems. I am happy to do so.

Don't be afraid to ask questions of them as well. When I interview directors, I always appreciate their inquiries about how we do things—it shows me that they want to know how we operate and often spurs me to remember things I forgot to cover.

If the theater pays—and sometimes theaters that don't normally pay their actors or other staff members do have a stipend for the director—don't be afraid to ask how much and when you will be paid. You're entitled to this information.

Ask about the uniqueness in the operation of the theater. Is their audition process out of the ordinary? Do they cast by committee or do you have the final word? Do they rehearse odd hours? Must you share the stage with construction crews or other activities? Are you expected to attend performances after the opening night or will a stage manager not only run the show but check up on its integrity?

In particular, you want to find out what is expected of you. This is a tricky area. Some theaters support the director with a whole slew of personnel, from a stage manager to an assistant director to a master carpenter and master electrician as well as the usual complement of designers, propsters, and set dressers. But other theaters expect the director to function in a great many capacities beyond "directing the actors" and "staging the show"—and you want to know this up front. It doesn't mean you won't accept a job where the director wears many hats, but you need to know.

Also, find out where the buck stops. In some theaters, the producer has the final say when a dispute arises, whether it is during the casting process; in a decision concerning a set, costume, lighting, or prop issue; or in making cuts to the material. In other theaters, the director has the final say and can overrule every other department or person. And then again, in some theaters, each department head has the final say—the set designer rules his domain, the choreographer has the final word on every dance, the costumer decides every costume detail, and the director is the final word only on staging and acting. I've worked in theaters using each of these chain-of-command methods, and any of them can work as long as you know going in what to expect. You might think that having the absolute final say on each issue is most desirable, but there can be instances when it is a good thing to have a third party, such as the producer, to decide the fate of an argument between for example, a director and a designer. A director needs to keep a happy family around him to ultimately be successful, and having the producer intercede can provide a good cop-bad cop scenario that will work in your favor.

What it really boils down to is this: if everyone working on the project is professional and reasonable and creative, and is totally clear on the director's vision, then issues can be worked out and everyone will bring something exciting to the table. But in an uneven creative environment, where you feel that one or more of the creative staff members is not up to their tasks, having the final say will prove beneficial. Short of that, if the producers share your vision, letting them intercede might work for you.

During the interview, be personable and forthcoming—I am always uncomfortable with a candidate who won't open up. When the person I am interviewing doesn't say much, I can't get a grasp of what he or she is thinking and often have to fill in the gaps—literally and figuratively—which can lead to inaccurate perceptions.

A word about perceptions—they can be much more persuasive than the truth! Not only in the interview stage, but also throughout the entire creative process, be careful that you are being perceived correctly. If a producer perceives you as being too egotistical; if an actor perceives you as not liking them; if a designer perceives you as being close-minded, it won't matter what the truth really is, you'll ultimately wind up having to do some damage control. Always be sensitive to what the perceptions are. In the interview, find the time to create the right perception about you and your work.

But be a good listener, too. Make the interviewer feel you are really paying attention to what he or she is saying. The producer may be trying to fill you in on the specific and often irregular procedures and methods of this particular theater, and if you indeed listen carefully, you can avoid a number of pitfalls later. You never want to be told when something goes amiss, "Well, I warned you at the very first interview . . ." If you are up against a somewhat verbose producer who likes to regale you with stories of past productions or personal triumphs, appear to listen intently. That will give the perception that you are fascinated—always a good thing. It's a fine art to know "when to talk" and "when to listen." Try to master it.

The bottom line is, always keep in mind that you are a salesperson trying to sell a very important product that may or may not have a lot of competition—*yourself!*

This package is made up of, in no particular order of importance:

- Your personality
- Your people skills
- Your creativity
- Your experience
- Your talent.

Your personality is what might win them over by assuring the producer that you will be able to work well within the organization. Your people skills will show that you can communicate your ideas both to other creative staff members and to performers while making them feel that their contribution to the production is paramount. Your creativity is what lets the producer know that you will deliver a five-star production that will please the board, the audience, the participants, and the critics. And having had a lot of experience is more impressive than not. But it is your talent that will ultimately make the difference between you and another director. If you have the innate talent to direct, you'll find that you'll be in demand.

Use everything in your stable to convey the above—in your manner and speech, in your support materials such as resumes and videotapes, and in your sense of excitement about this project and theater in general. That can be infectious, and is perhaps your strongest selling point of all.

Where Are the Jobs?

How do you go about finding what jobs are available? If you are in an area where there are only one or two theaters within a reasonable commute, the answer is obvious. But if there are dozens of theaters to try and approach in your area, or if you are looking to branch out and work throughout the country, then you need to do some research.

I remember—not too long ago—when the local papers were the only source of information. One large daily paper would list auditions every Wednesday, which would give an idea of which theaters were doing what. But times have changed, and the Internet is really your best source now.

Almost every theater has a website or some sort of presence on the Internet. Finding the theaters is fairly simple—merely go to Google or another search engine and type in the name of the town you are researching and the word *theater*. You'll be amazed at what comes up. You'll have to separate the movie theaters from the legitimate theaters, but you'll find what you're looking for. You can find theaters by searching their names or by searching a town's website for entertainment venues.

There are also a lot of chat rooms, message boards, and newsgroups devoted to local theaters, and sometimes you can find information about the quality of the theaters as well. Message boards can and should serve the local theaters as a forum for exchanging ideas, promoting shows, trading sets and props, and encouraging business.

If you are trying to have a professional career as a director, there is a publication to which you must subscribe. It is accessible in an online version, updated every three business days, and in a print version, published twice monthly. It is called *ArtSEARCH: The National Employment Bulletin for the Arts*. Their URL is www.tcg.org /frames/artsearch/fs_artsearch.htm. It is published by the Theater Communications Group and lists jobs in every area of the performing arts. Well worth the investment!

Let me leave you with this last thought—the most successful directors are those who know their strengths and weaknesses. They know the niche in which they fit. As an example, when I first began to direct at Plays-in-the-Park, I did two well-received and reviewed Sondheim musicals in a row, *Sweeney Todd* and *Follies*. Despite their success, it was not "a given" that I would be asked back to direct for a third year because the producer had quite a large stable of directors to choose from. At the interview for the upcoming summer season, I was offered *South Pacific*. I very much wanted to direct a show that summer, but I politely turned the offer down, explaining that I simply wasn't the right director for the project—that I had no true affinity for the vehicle and therefore felt that I would not bring any unique "take" to the production. While I knew I could most likely mount an adequate production, it wouldn't have the spark that the two prior shows had because they were the type of shows

I was willing to devote a year of my life to. When I considered the research I knew I would spend time on for months prior, the pre-production work that I devote to the details, and the six weeks of rehearsals, I felt it more important to wait for the right show rather than risk both the success of the production and my own happiness. Had this been a high school production or one for a small community theater I might have tried my hand at it—after all, a director needs to expand and grow too, but there was too much at stake at this particular theater. It turned out to be a wise choice, because I was offered *A Little Night Music* the following summer, and ultimately became the producing director of the theater.

By knowing what you are good at, where your strengths lie, and what type of show inspires you, you'll approach each project with the necessary excitement to create art. That excitement will carry over into the interview as well—it will be infectious to the producer. There is absolutely nothing wrong with being known as a director who is great at Shakespeare, or can handle large musicals, or has a knack for slapstick comedy. It will make producers seek you out.

Of course, in your "formative years" you need to try your hand at a lot of show styles until you find your niche, and I encourage that, as long as the experimentation suits the style, size, and mission of the theater.

2

What to Expect from Each Type of Theater

I feel it's important to go into some detail about each type of venue you find yourself working in, giving my experience. It is not meant to be definitive or conclusive since each theater will have its own idiosyncrasies and uniqueness, but perhaps it will give you an idea of what to look for and what to look out for. Take or leave the advice as you wish. It is purely my opinion.

High School Theater

I'd like to preface my discussion on directing at the high school level by stating emphatically that there is no better venue to hone your directing skills. Too often high school plays and musicals carry a stigma of being amateurish and unworthy of a serious director's attention, but nothing could be further from the truth. In fact, high school is the perfect place to develop your rapport with actors, refine your ability to interact with management, and test your creativity in solving a myriad of theatrical problems—from technical limitations to adapting the material to your performer base. And you can do all this within a safe environment and supportive atmosphere where your audience is predisposed to embrace your work.

The creativity you develop and techniques you perfect while working with high school actors, not to mention your enhanced organizational and interpersonal skills in dealing with the powers that be—whoever they are—will prepare you in so many ways for all the other potential types of theaters you might work at. And you just might find, as I have, that directing on a high school level does not have to be merely a stepping-stone to more professional theaters, but rather a challenge and a reward unto itself. The thirty-plus shows I've directed at Cranford High School are among my fondest. "Professional" is not always a legal term, it is also a state of mind and state of heart.

For the past fifteen years I have directed the straight play in the fall and the musical in the spring at Cranford High School in Cranford, New Jersey. I feel eminently competent to talk about high school theater because of this experience, but keep in mind that high schools can be distinctly different from place to place. During my tenure at CHS I initially shared the directing duties of the straight play with the English teacher, but after about five seasons he left and I did it on my own.

High school students are extremely eager to learn and to please and, unlike experienced performers, who may be slightly jaded, they are willing to try anything. This is particularly rewarding with a musical where you might even get boys to dance who would, perhaps, be more reluctant to try as they get older. I've also found that I can continue to make changes throughout the rehearsal period and most of the kids will be able to keep up and adapt. Only a handful will not be able to change what they have learned from the very first day, but this can be true of performers on all levels.

Sometimes you need to be aware that a high school show might be more about the "event" than the artistic quality of the show. Very often parents like to get involved. Sometimes this is a good thing—they can help build and paint sets, sew costumes, gather props, and help with publicity. Other times they may tend to interfere somewhat so you'll want to establish the ground rules up front before enlisting parental assistance.

Depending on the school and the emphasis they place on theater, a director is sometimes faced with having to pad the cast with as many bodies as possible. Some high schools wish to get as many students involved as possible because this can translate to large audiences and more money at the box office. Schools that place emphasis on the educational value of theater will look more for an artistic success even if the show doesn't pack the house.

Opting for a huge cast happens mostly with musicals (it is nearly impossible to pad *The Odd Couple*, for example—just how many card players can one living room hold?). It can be a daunting challenge for both the director and choreographer to create balanced stage pictures and share stage time. If you find yourself with this task, always suggest large musicals with large choruses whenever possible. Shows with huge ensembles can certainly be fun, but I would caution the director and choreographer to be judicious in the way the crowds are used. Not everyone has to dance—an ensemble of onlookers who just sing is common practice even on Broadway.

One possible solution to retaining the original cast size of a show and still get as many people involved as possible is to "double cast" the production, but this can result twice as much work for the creative team and, sometimes, a competitive atmosphere.

Casting itself can be challenging, again depending on the school's policies. Some schools give you the freedom to cast whoever is right for the role, while other schools might go with the hierarchy theory—seniors get the leads, juniors supporting roles, and down the line. Fight for true open casting, even if that means you have to calm an irate parent or two. Obviously, if two actors are truly equal and one is a senior you might lean in that direction, but if it is clear-cut that a sophomore is right for a lead, trust your instincts and your integrity will win out.

I have generally found that in high school casting (and indeed mounting) the show is much more of a group effort than in a community theater. At the high school where I work there is the director (me) and a choreographer (Michelle, who has been my partner for as long as I have been there). We both were hired from outside the school system. Internally, there is the head of the music department who always serves as the producer but has conducted the orchestra as well; the choral director who teaches the vocals; the band director who conducts the orchestra; and the art teacher who oversees the painting of the sets and props. Over the years there has occasionally also been any or all of the following: the shop teacher who did the sets (in-house); an outside designer who built the sets with the students; the home economics teacher who used her sewing class to make costumes (in-house); a costume coordinator who rented all the costumes (in-house and outside hire); student stage managers (in-house) and adult stage managers (outside hire); and an A/V teacher who did the lighting (in-house) and outside lighting designers; scenic artists who painted and students who painted; and both in-house and outside piano players who served as rehearsal pianists and pit keyboardists. Each season is different, but as long as you know what's going on right at the start and every person's job description is clear, it works out. Every September I send a long email to the department head outlining the specific needs for the two shows (which are usually picked before school is out the year prior) and we start to work on our staffing needs.

If you are directing the nonmusical, the job is often easier because there is no need for musicians, most shows are comprised of a single set, and the cast is often smaller. Generally, this means the audience will be smaller as well, but if the school is producing the straight play as part of an arts education program, this should not have any major consequences.

For the past few years I have done something a little different at the high school—I have directed a minimusical in the fall instead of a straight play. At first, I had mixed feelings about this because it precluded those students who are serious dramatic and comedic actors without musical talent. For this reason, I would not suggest a steady diet of musicals.

The first year I tried it I did *Working,* based on Studs Terkel's book, with music by Stephen Schwartz and James Taylor, among others. The next year I did *The Fantasticks* (both licensed through Music Theater International, a.k.a. MTI). Both years it worked out very well and was an exciting experience for the small cast of actors and the audience.

There was no budget for a live orchestra, so I employed a very talented composer/musician who is also quite adept at synthesizers and sequencers—Mark Baron, the composer of *Frankenstein, the Musical,* which I cowrote (shameless plug—www.frankensteinthemusical.com). He was able to take the scores provided by MTI (*The Fantasticks* was scored for piano, harp, drums, and bass; in *Working* there were seven orchestra parts: two keyboards, electric/acoustic guitar, bass, percussion, drums, and various woodwinds) and play each part into his sequencer. I asked Mark how he went about it, since playing "Sweet Home, Alabama" on the guitar is about all I can do, and here is his quote:

> The process goes like this:
> The musical director must have a computer-based sequencing program: Pro-tools, Cakewalk, Sonar, Cubass, etc. The process is much too big to be done on a sequencer built into a keyboard—even the most up-to-date sequencing keyboards don't have nearly the amount of data storage.

Sequence all the orchestra parts: This is a very time-consuming step . . . the larger the orchestra the tougher the job.

If you are going to then play back from the computer, it is very important that the sound source you use is as authentic as possible. If the sequence is played back using the computer sound card or an inadequate keyboard you will not get a product that is useable. Instead you will get something that sounds more like a video game rather than an orchestra. This is due to the lack of expression, dynamics, etc., that are not possible with many low-end keyboards.

Once you have the parts recorded, you need to set the sequence to the show. Setting tempos is tricky. Instead of setting a song at one tempo, you need to get the sequence to breathe like live performers. Live performers (singers and musicians) move the tempo just a bit. This needs to be done to make your sequence more "Human." The best thing to do is understand the singer who is performing the song and try to emulate his or her style and strong points. If you set the song to one tempo the listener will get an unnatural feeling and the sequence will in turn hurt rather than help you.

If the score is going to be run from a CD/MD rather than a computer for performances, you need to set all the vamps in the show. Because of this you want to get the final product to the performers as quickly as possible.

It is my hope that any musician reading the above will understand it better than I do, but I can assure the reader that it works surprisingly well. While nothing can replace the excitement of live musicians (or the expense—oops, did I say that?) there is also a lot to be said for the consistency of tempos, the ability to control the volume, and the lack of any sour notes that you get when you sequence the music.

Let me also add that MTI offers MIDI-orchestrations for many of their musicals in the event the high school director does not have access to a Mark Baron. These tracks are piano only—there are no orchestrations, but MTI also offers OrchExtra, which are sequenced tracks. This solution would work for any type of theater that does not utilize union musicians, and all it takes is cassette or CD copies of the recorded tracks that each actor listens to relentlessly to become familiar with every nuance of the sequenced music. Some actors take to the recorded music with ease, while others find it difficult. Additional rehearsal time needs to be allotted, and the actors need to work on their own with the CDs or tapes as well.

Here's a situation unique to high school theater—scheduling. Scheduling can be an issue in every type of theater except Equity, but high school scheduling encompasses some unique challenges. First, there is the scheduling of the show itself. Every town seems to present their show in the first two weeks of March, and while you won't draw much outside your town, if shows can be somewhat staggered, you can increase the audience base plus allow your students to see what the other schools are doing.

Worse, however, is trying to schedule in a town where not only the high school but other schools are doing shows as well. Here it really is beneficial to try to meet with everyone concerned and draw up a reasonable calendar a year in advance.

Finally, unless your school has an enormous number of students, you'll be casting kids who also have jobs, sports, cheerleading, debating, band practice, SATs and a slew of clubs to which they belong. There's no easy way to deal with it except clever scheduling and a combination of after-school and evening rehearsals. Just be aware that it is something to contend with.

It becomes a directorial decision: to go with the most talented actors and deal with the conflicts or to choose a conflict-free cast of actors who might not comprise your first-choice performers. It is a dilemma, and a decision that directors can face at every level of theater. Do you wait for Tom Cruise to free up his schedule or do you go with Murray Lapinksy?

As far as the scenery, costumes, props, and lighting are concerned, it's a crapshoot. Sometimes you'll be lucky and there will be teachers or students or parents willing to head up each department. Sometimes you won't be so lucky and you'll spend 24/7 doing everything yourself. Be prepared for either contingency.

For scenery, there is a company, ScenoGraphics, that can provide easy-to-understand plans for a great many set designs. I know a lot of people who have used their designs and are quite happy with them. They're worth a look. They can be found online at www.scenographics.com, and, in addition to their "Design-Paks," they can provide you with show T-shirts, posters, banners, and even muslin.

With respect to costuming, over the past ten years or so I have noticed a change in the high school where I work. There used to be a sewing class that would tackle the costuming as part of their class assignments. That faded away to a sewing club. That faded to oblivion. I think sewing is a lost art, and while you'll find classes in high school and college for design, homemaking-style sewing is rare. If the budget is there, rent the costumes—you'll be better off in the long run. Some schools have the students provide their own costumes. Economical for the school, costly for the kids, and could result in a very noncohesive and eclectic design!

Lighting seems to take care of itself on a high school level in that either the theater is terribly underequipped and some wonderful, nerdish student (no offence to techno-kids!) will know how to turn the few instruments on and off, or the high school will be marvelously equipped and a nerdish teacher along with several nerdish students will work miracles.

Whenever possible, encourage the creation of various clubs relating to theater—a lighting club, a costume club, and so on. The more people you get involved the easier your job is—at least, that's the hope.

I truly feel that excellent theater can be done on a high school level, and the director's goal is to train young performers in the art of theater and its disciplines while encouraging, coaxing, and cajoling them into the best possible performances. The phrase "just a high school show" should be banned from our vocabulary. Each spring I am amazed—and pleased—at how many of the students whom I have worked with for the prior four years are accepted into enviable colleges and universities with majors in theater. I can't help but feel partly responsible because I took my directing job—and high school theater—very seriously.

Rehearsal and performance schedules: High school shows can rehearse for as long as eight weeks or more, mostly after school, Saturday morning, and some evenings. This depends on many variables, especially whether the stage is free or being used for other activities. The shows usually consist of three or four performances over a weekend, sometimes adding a Thursday night preview and a matinee or two. Sometimes they run for a second weekend.

Pay: High schools can be most generous in their pay scales, particularly if you have worked there for a number of years. It is not unusual for a director who has worked at the same high school season after season to reach $3,000 or more per show; in fact, raises are frequently built in to the stipend. But directors starting out with their first show at a high school in a low- or middle-income area might make far less. Sometimes it is tied to what coaches and other extracurricular facilitators are paid, but not always.

College Theater

If high school theater is consumed with the event, college theater can be mired in academia. This does not, by any means, have to be a bad thing, but as with any theatrical endeavor, the more you are prepared and enlightened, the easier and more creative the project will be. To borrow from a national clothing store's motto: an educated director is the best director.

I have been brought in as a guest director on a number of college productions—most notably a new work about the AIDS Quilt (*Quilt*, licensed through MTI), as well as other obscure and well-known pieces. Each project was different in terms of casting and production values, but the one pervasive theme throughout each college production was the fact that an aura of education or learning permeated. In addition to getting down to the business of producing the show, each step in the process had to be explained or "taught" to the students, many of whom were receiving credit toward their courses by working on the show. So the director served as a teacher as well. This can actually be fun and help sharpen and define your own methods and philosophies, but occasionally there can be conflicts if the director's methods don't quite gel with the curriculum or syllabus of, say, the scene design instructor or the technical director.

There are plenty of professors who pride themselves in keeping up with the times; theater equipment—especially lighting and sound—advances almost as quickly as computers. Yesterday's technology can become outdated a year later. But there are just as many who refuse to move with the times and are locked in the ways they were taught twenty or thirty years ago. I'm not editorializing—well, at least not too much—just preparing you.

Otherwise, working in college theater was a thrill. Often the facilities are state-of-the-art. The students on both sides of the curtain are usually majoring in theater and so are kindred spirits. Budgets are frequently ample. Experimentation is encouraged, and it is not unusual to be able to direct a show that is not regularly done on a community theater level, let alone a high school level. For me, there is something almost religious about sitting in a modern, steel-and-cement university theater—a feeling that is quite different from most other venues. The Vivian Beaumont Theater at Lincoln Center in New York is the best example I can give of what a modern university theater feels like; if you were ever in that theater you'll understand the reference. The theater itself feels fresh and experimental and exciting and challenging and clean, as if this is a place where art and technology fuse to form something thrilling.

College theater is an excellent place to hone your craft and enjoy the freedom to indulge your creativity. Because it is under the umbrella of academia (instead of the burden of ticket sales), innovation is often not only accepted but also welcomed, and sometimes expected. The luxury of being less dependant on a box office can allow for productions of lesser-known works or works that deserve to be seen but might not be commercial blockbusters.

I found that the college students cast in the show took their craft—and themselves—very seriously and worked hard. An inspiring director will often form a very tight bond with his cast, and I discovered that they are game for any changes and risks you might wish to throw at them. The "techies" usually work very hard as well, and seem to enjoy their tasks. College simply happens to be a fun place, and drama students see their college years as an opportunity to work and grow and even "make connections" to the professional world. If the opportunity comes your way to be a guest director at a college with a good drama department, by all means accept!

Rehearsal and performance schedules: I have rehearsed from eight weeks down to three weeks, sometimes during the day, sometimes at night, sometimes on weekends, depending on space and whether the production is done as part of a class or series of classes, or is extracurricular. The performance schedule is similar to high school, although I have experienced special matinees for high school students and senior groups, and have even enjoyed runs spanning two or three weekends.

Pay: Anywhere from $1,000 to $2,500 in my experience.

Community Theater

Community theater—much more than high school or college theater—is a social animal. My first book was titled *The Community
Theater Handbook;* it is an area I know quite well. It is possibly the
type of theater many readers of this book will work at most often.

The reason I call community theater a social animal is that a
great many community theaters are generations old, and they are
looked upon as a huge extended family. There are even committees
whose entire function is to provide refreshments and organize din-
ners, parties, and so on. This is not to say that there isn't good work
happening at community theaters—far from it. There can be great
work done at this level. But it is the director's job—dare I say,
duty—to set the standard for the group and make sure that the
quality is top-notch.

The actors who audition for shows at a community theater are
a decidedly mixed bag. On one extreme you will get performers who
are very, very serious about their craft, with the highest standards of
discipline. At Plays-in-the-Park—a community theater—we have
had several actors graduate to leading roles in Broadway shows. The
next tier comprises those performers who do not have aspirations
for professional theater but look to do the best work possible in the
best shows. They might be any age, from high school to senior citi-
zen. Quite often they have had a lot of experience at local theaters
and, while they enjoy the social aspects, they are ready and willing
to work hard. The next tier is one variation between the two extremes,
on the other end of the spectrum you have those performers who
are really more interested in either finding a date through the
rehearsal process or merely enjoy the after-rehearsal activities of
going out for late-night suppers or bar-hopping with the cast. Again,
I'm not editorializing—and as long as you are aware of these folks,
you won't be disappointed in their behavior.

If you set the ground rules right up front—and enforce them—
you should get along with all sorts of actors. I most often begin the
first rehearsal by explaining, gently but firmly, that for the three or
four hours they are at rehearsal, they are on my time. What they do
before they get to rehearsal and what they do afterward is their
time; but as long as they are here, they are mine. I expect that during rehearsal hours their concentration will be solely on rehearsals.
I don't mind levity and a relaxed atmosphere, as long as the work

gets done. By setting the tone from the start, the varying types of performers generally will mesh well. In fact, I have found that quite often the professional attitude and approach by the more serious actors will rub off on the others, but only if everyone knows from the beginning what you expect.

Community theaters also vary dramatically in what they expect of the director. Some theaters will provide you with set, lighting, and costume designers who are supported by worker bees to do the construction, electrical work, and creation of the costumes. Other theaters expect that you will bring along your own roster of designers and seek volunteers for the busy work. Some community theaters will provide a stage manager who actually is familiar with what a stage manager does, while others will assign an "assistant director," which is usually a euphemism for someone who will spend most of their time giving lines to actors when they stumble, but won't be of great help in writing down your blocking and other needs. And some community theaters will provide you with a producer from the board members for your show (some even have a permanent producer) who will be your liaison among the designers, and will troubleshoot the whole process for you, while other theaters more or less expect you to produce as well as direct.

It is the wise director who knows ahead of time the peculiarities of the theater that has hired him or her. As long as you know what you are getting into, you can choose whether this theater—and its methodology—is a right place for you.

While high schools rehearse and perform more often than not in the high school auditorium, and colleges usually have at least one main stage theater, and sometimes two or three additional smaller venues or black-box spaces,[1] community theaters sometimes do not have a permanent home of their own. I have worked

---

1 A black-box theater space is a catchall phrase for a room in which the stage and the seating arrangements constantly change from production to production. Often there is a crisscrossing grid of pipe secured above to hang lights on in any configuration, a stage made of platforms that can be moved and rearranged, and temporary seating on risers. Black-box spaces lend themselves easily to theater-in-the-round, three-quarter thrust stages, and everything in between. While generally used for experimental works and minimal cast dramas and comedies, I have seen, and directed, full-scale musicals in black-box theaters of all sizes.

at community theaters that took up residence on the stage of a local church or temple, utilized a converted barn, mounted shows at the high school and at the middle school, borrowed spaces from colleges, used an Elks meeting hall, and performed outside in parks. I have also worked at community theaters that do indeed own their own structures—from churches they have purchased to newly designed concrete-and-steel stand-alone buildings. That's one of the neat things about community theaters—they make theaters out of almost anything. In the mid-seventies, I founded a community theater that began in the lower-level catering hall of a bar and then moved to a deserted feed-and-seed store.

Rehearsal and performance schedules: Rehearsing anywhere from six to eight weeks is common, most often evenings and weekends (since most people have other jobs). Community theaters might stretch the runs out over several weekends (Thursday through Sunday, with a matinee or two), or do it all at once, as in the case of Plays-in-the-Park (an outdoor summer theater) which does ten consecutive performances of each show.

Pay: Sometimes nothing at all, but at those theaters that do pay the directors, it can range anywhere from a few hundred dollars to $1,500 or more. Fortunately for readers of this book, if anyone is to be paid at a community theater, it usually is the director. Sometimes, when a stipend is not offered, expenses will be reimbursed by the theater.

Semi-Professional Regional Theaters

Of all the types of theaters, semiprofessional regional theaters afford the director the most professional environment in which to work. This is not to say that the actual productions are guaranteed to be better than those at colleges and community theaters—I have seen brilliant work done by amateurs and mediocrity presented by professionals—but the conditions in which you rehearse tend to be of a higher level.

For purposes of this book, a semiprofessional regional theater is defined as a theater in a permanent home (even if it is leased at a college or other venue) offering a season of shows utilizing at least some Equity actors and an Equity stage manager. For information on the union of American theatrical actors and stage managers, Actor's Equity Association, go to: www.actorsequity.org/home.html.

I have worked recently in two such theaters—one is permanently located in a renovated movie theater and does two or three main stage plays and musicals a year while producing weekly children's shows during the day or weekends to make ends meet. The other is housed in a nicely appointed theater that is part of a museum, and they do four or five shows each season, mostly nonmusicals with the occasional small musical thrown in.

These theaters work under agreements where at least half the cast and the stage manager must be members of Equity. They hire designers and construction crews as needed. Both have a permanent technical director to oversee and coordinate lighting, sets, props, and costumes. One employs a resident lighting designer. Both theaters have an artistic director, and this person acts as producer for every show, giving continuity to the productions. Depending on the theater, the artistic director might answer to a governing board in terms of budget and sometimes for approval of play selections. Ideally this should be as close to a professional situation as you will encounter. The next step up would be full Equity regional theaters like Yale Rep in Connecticut—and from there, of course, national tours, on Broadway, and off Broadway.

Rehearsal and performance schedules: Your rehearsal schedule will be governed by Equity rules, and the stage manager will coordinate it. Generally, it is two or three weeks (since time is money) and rehearsals would be held during the day with appropriate breaks. Right before you open you are allowed one or two 10-out-of-12 rehearsals, meaning you can work a pretty long day! A 10-out-of-12 allows for ten hours of straight rehearsal time with lunch and dinner breaks. Performance schedules vary at these theaters, from four to eight performances a week for several weeks, although shorter runs are possible as well.

Pay: This type of regional theater is often struggling to make ends meet, because they are a hybrid between a good community theater and a full-fledged Equity house. I have found that $1,500 for a director is about average, but that's only my experience. I just don't know what they pay in Boise or Salt Lake City or Los Angeles.

Hopefully I have provided an overview of the various levels of theater where you might find work. Each has its pros and cons, and each is capable of exciting and terrific theater. Now that you know how to sell yourself and have a sense of the four potential venues where you might be able to direct, let's assume you've gotten a job. Mazel tov.

3

Research

As soon as I have been hired to direct a certain play or musical, my research begins, even before preproduction involving any of the other collaborators. The first step is to become familiar with the genre of the piece. A play or musical can fall into any number of styles of theater, not just the headings of comedy, drama, and musical. Within the nonmusical world there are many genres: farce, melodrama, documentary, mystery, classical, Shakespearean (not really a genre but certainly a style), experimental, romantic, gothic, and combinations of all of the above.

Musicals can also have subgenres such as pop opera, operetta, musical revue, dance show (such as *Movin' Out* and *Contact*), musical melodrama—in fact, you can even make a case for delineating the old-style shows of Rodgers and Hammerstein and Cole Porter from the newer shows of Stephen Sondheim and Andrew Lloyd Webber, or the small off-Broadway style shows from the big, splashy Broadway type.

Once you've defined the genre and style of the show, you will want to find and develop an approach that suits theme. To do this, it would be helpful to research and/or see other shows that fall into the same style. If you are directing *Murder Among Friends*, a murder-mystery melodrama, watch the movies *Deathtrap* and *Sleuth*. If you are directing *The Importance of Being Earnest*, seek out other plays by Oscar Wilde and study the time period—London in 1895. Someone directing *Pirates of Penzance* will want to study the style of Gilbert and Sullivan.

Every genre has a rich history and a style that it evokes, and unless you are intentionally rejecting that style in an attempt at doing something unique or experimental, you'll want to be completely familiar and comfortable within the style. In fact, you can't very well deconstruct something until you know all about it, so research pays off regardless. Familiarity and comfort with the style can help you fall in love with it, or at the very least, respect it. It is important, as a director, for you to have a fondness for the material. If you've ever worked with a director who doesn't like the show and is doing it for the money or other nonartistic reasons, you probably found the experience trying at best. But if you work with a director who is inspired and thrilled to be doing a particular show, the feeling becomes contagious and inspires everyone else, from the cast to the crew to the audience.

After you've developed a feeling for the genre of work, it's time to move on to the research for the specific show you are going to direct. Let's say you're set to helm a production of Frank Wildhorn's musical version of *Jekyll and Hyde*. I would want to become an authority on everything to do with the show itself, its source material, the time period it is set in, and anything else I can discover in my quest. After all, I am going to have to steer a choreographer; a musical director; set, lighting, and costume designers; a prop artisan; a stage manager; and a slew of actors into creating the best possible version of this show given the resources, venue, and talent available. Plus, I am going to have to make the producer or board members happy—I want to be asked back.

I didn't get a chance, let's say, to see the show on Broadway, nor do I have the cast album (I know it's now a CD, but cast album sounds better). So my first step would be to see what's out there from the original musical. I don't have to leave my house—I merely fire up my computer, log on, and point my browser to Amazon.com.

Wow. There's a lot of material out there. I have easily found (1) the original broadway cast album with Robert Cuccioli, (2) a DVD of a televised version with David Hasselhoff, (3) the sheet music for the songs complete with photos of the original show, (4) a 1994 concept cast recording that appears to have some different songs than the OBC (Original Broadway Cast) recording, (5) the book *The Strange Case of Dr. Jekyll* by Robert Louis Stevenson (ah . . . the source material!) as well as (5.5) the Cliffs Notes, plus (6) a DVD double feature of the two original movies—one with Fredric March and one with Spencer Tracy. There are also plenty more entries, but it seems these are the most viable—I doubt very much I need the DVD of *Dr. Jekyll and Sister Hyde,* or a gift certificate to the Jekyll and Hyde restaurant in Greenwich Village.

If I add up the cost of the first six items (I'll read the whole book and skip Cliffs Notes) I find I'm about to invest about $100. Well, that qualifies for free shipping and no tax, so what the heck, I order it all. While I'm waiting for my shipment, I do a general Google search for Jekyll and Hyde.

Again, I'm rewarded with tons of information. There are a number of sites dedicated to the show itself with all sorts of insight into the pre-Broadway tour, the Broadway show, and the post-Broadway tour. I wasn't aware that the show went through so many revisions—but if I'm to become an authority, I'll need to study them all. There are also scholarly sites dedicated to a study of the original novel, discussing at great length the good versus evil basis for the story. Hey, there's even a site for that restaurant in New York.

I have yet another ace up my sleeve for research, a mail-order company called Package Publicity Service:

Package Publicity Service, Inc.
(212) 255-2872
255 West 88th Street, #3E
New York, NY 10024-1716

This organization carries everything needed to promote the show, including legal-to-use show logos in various sizes (some are a tad corny but most of them are the original artwork), posters, and press books. I'm interested in the press book because I know that it contains not only the reviews from every major New York paper, but copies of the original cast breakdown, scene breakdown, and song list from the original Playbill. Maybe I can talk the producer into paying for this. The producer can use the information for the program as well as for press releases sent to local newspapers to advertise the show. I can use the press book to see exactly how many were in the original show—I don't want to pad the ensemble but I want to make sure all the supporting and character roles are covered. The original script and the original Playbill will also tell you the cast size.

The Press Books contain the various New York and out-of-town reviews of the original production, and reviews of the pre-Broadway and subsequent tours are often included. Here you can find out what the critics liked and didn't like, and why some things might have been changed. Dig deeper and you'll sometimes find descriptions of choreography or set designs or lighting concepts that will help you with your production. A valuable resource indeed!

To complete my initial research materials (as I delve further, I'll branch out on the Internet to study the time period, the costumes, the social climate, etc.), I'll see if the producer has put in a call to the licensing company, Music Theater International, to ask them to send to the theater a perusal copy of the libretto (script), the score, and the chorus book. Most licensing companies will send you this material to look over for about two weeks, provided you pay a security deposit and the postage. Since this is the material I will ultimately be working from, it's the most important of all. Normally the librettos and one or two conductor's scores come about eight weeks prior to the show's opening, and the orchestra parts come about a month before (you can have everything earlier; however, you'll pay extra), but I want to study everything ahead of time.

It is illegal to Xerox the material—and I wouldn't suggest doing anything illegal. Having a photographic memory helps. Reading the libretto a zillion times in two weeks also helps. In a few cases, mostly with Samuel French, you can actually buy the librettos, either from French itself or from a store like the Drama Book Shop (www.dramabookshop.com). On some shows, French requires you to buy the librettos; they cannot be rented.

There used to be a wonderful service that sold hardcover scripts for most shows and musicals through the mail—the Fireside Theater Book Club, which was later known as Stage and Screen— but they went out of business a few years ago. I have a collection of over 160 hardcover scripts—many complete with photos—dating back from the days when I worked as an assistant and legit theater agent at the William Morris Agency in the seventies. It's sad that they are no longer available, although I would imagine a search on eBay might turn up any number of them.

Okay—the perusal copies have arrived, and so has the material from Amazon. It's a daunting task, but now the process of absorbing and analyzing all the research begins. How you attack all the material is up to you—but since I'm the author, here's what I would do.

I want to read the original novel first. I basically know the story, but it will be fascinating for me to have the classic story line fresh in my mind as I discover what the creators of the musical have kept, discarded, and, well, distorted. Having done that, the next step would be to read the libretto. What I like to do is keep a CD player alongside the couch I'm curled up on, and when I get to a song in the libretto, I'll play the CD and follow along. In fact, if there's an overture, I'll play that before I even open the script. In the case of *Jekyll and Hyde*, I notice a number of discrepancies between the original cast album and the libretto MTI has provided, but that's all part of my discovery process, and I'm sure I'll be able to distinguish the various versions as I keep exploring.

The next step will be to compare the video with the libretto and the cast album. I'm somewhat lucky—very few shows are video-taped professionally (there's a black market for bootlegged tapes of shows, shot mostly by someone in the audience holding a wobbly camcorder, but let's not go there) and I can probably count them on both hands—*Sweeney Todd; Into the Woods; Sunday in the Park with George; Passion; Gypsy* (with Bette Midler); *Putting It Together* (all Stephen Sondheim—yeah!); *Jesus Christ, Superstar; Cats; Joseph and the Amazing Technicolor Dreamcoat* (all Andrew Lloyd Webber); *Oklahoma* (with Hugh Jackman); *Pippin; Fosse; Barnum; Kiss Me, Kate; Smokey Joe's Café*—okay, three hands. And if you search terribly hard, you might find a copy of *Something's Afoot, Philemon*, and *The Robber Bridegroom*, recorded when Showtime had a Broadway series.

I'm sure there are even more, but my point is, there are precious few. For the most part, what we have are movies made from the musical, and movie musicals can stray from the original quite a bit. Shot-on-video Broadway musicals can give you the best possible feeling of what the show looked and sounded like, and while I'm not suggesting that they be replicated beat for beat, I cannot stress more emphatically the value in seeing how the show was originally conceived by the authors and original creative staff.

Movie musicals, on the other hand, can give you the flavor of the time period and an idea of the show, but you must always remember it is a movie—opened up, cut back or elongated, and in other ways changed. The film of *Cabaret*—while brilliant in its own right—takes a very different approach than the Hal Prince Broadway show, or the Studio 54 revival. Occasionally a movie is close to the original—such as the old *Li'l Abner* movie or even *1776*, but generally they are "Hollywoodized"—still very valuable as a research tool, but only in feeling and flavor.

Back to the video of *Jekyll and Hyde*—seeing it is very helpful. Experiencing the show, as opposed to just listening to it, gives me the opportunity to visualize how the show plays on a stage with real actors and production values, and lets me viscerally experience what I think will work and what I think might not in my particular venue.

I now have a terrific understanding of the show. My research has taken me from the original source material to the original cast recording, to the script I will be using, to a video representation of the play. I further refine my comprehension by listening to the "concept" album, which provides me with songs that were cut, songs that were added, and some different interpretations of those that stayed from the beginning.

It has been a welcome trend throughout the years for classic shows to be reinterpreted on CD—often restoring original songs and incidental music that didn't fit when a 33 1/3 RPM record was the only recording medium (show of hands—how many people remember records? How many still have a turntable and a collection? I do). If one of these newly recorded CDs is available for your project, by all means get it and listen to it. As you'll most likely be rehearsing with a single piano, these CDs can let you hear what the whole orchestra will sound like, helping with your staging and choreography. Often you'll want to accent movement to the percussion, and without the CD you'd have to wait until the orchestra rehearses before you are made aware of all the percussive accents. Even if you won't be using a full orchestra, chances are good you'll have a drummer (playing a trap set of bass drum, snare drum, tom tom, and a high hat and crash cymbal) and a percussionist who plays the mallet instruments such as tympani, xylophone, congas, cowbell, orchestra bells, marimba, triangle, and other sound effects. These fully orchestrated and revitalized new CDs will help a lot in understanding what is to come during tech week when the orchestra is added.

To round out my research, I'll watch the double feature of *Jekyll and Hyde* movies, to see how others interpreted the characters and to get any other little tidbits to file away. Maybe there's something I can use, perhaps even to pay homage to these classic films.

Last of all, I'll turn to the Internet to study the time period— London in the 1800s—so that I can talk intelligently about the clothing, the upper and lower classes, the look of the architecture and transportation—anything and everything that will allow me to submerge myself in the period.

I was lucky with *Jekyll and Hyde*—there was a wealth of information out there for me to embrace. Not every show will have so much, but regardless, you'll want to grab anything you can. And this quest for knowledge is not limited to musicals. With straight plays you'll find literary criticism on the Internet. You can read other works by the author. You can look up reviews. Use your imagination. Oh, and there's one more step. If the play is being produced anywhere around you—go see it. You can get a lot of helpful information from a great production. You can get even more from a lousy one.

4

The Concept

Now that you are an expert on the show at hand, you have to make a major decision before you begin preproduction meetings with your staff of designers. This decision may have, indeed, been already made by the producer—in fact, it might be why you were hired—but let's assume for the moment that it hasn't been decided yet. It is whether to approach the production in such a way that it is as true as possible to the original or to attempt a reinterpretation. And, of course, there is the third option of choosing to ignore all previous versions and use the script solely as your inspiration. This subject seems to be a sore point among a great many directors. I tend to be a purist, and my opinions may rankle some readers, but for what they are worth, here are my thoughts.

I favor giving the audience an experience as close to what was seen on Broadway whenever possible, and here are my reasons:

- If you are conducting a symphony by Beethoven, you don't make it sound or feel like the Dixie Chicks. Beethoven has proven himself worthy of having his work heard the way he wrote the piece.
- Audiences outside of New York or other big cities where road tours play do not get to see Broadway productions and, as members of the theater community, we owe it to them to try to re-create the experience.
- The authors and creators of an established hit have turned the written word into a hit because of what they created— why mess with that?

- In almost all cases, radically altering the script is against your licensing agreement.

- In some cases, such as with *Fiddler on the Roof*, you are bound by your licensing agreement to re-create the original choreography.

- Many fledgling directors just don't have the theatrical savvy to successfully reinvent a show.

Now, having said that, there are a number of instances where it is simply not possible or desirable to re-create the original concept, and then reinterpretation is necessary:

- The theater is simply too small or too ill equipped to do anything but a pared-down version of the show.

- The producer has specifically requested that the show be done in some different way.

- As part of a college course or as an "experimental alternative series" at a theater, the whole point of producing a show is to creatively revisit it.

- The show, by its very nature, is open to interpretation.

Of course I am referring primarily to Broadway-style musicals and very conceptual nonmusicals. *Romeo and Juliet* is rarely staged like the original (we now use women in our shows!). Each director freshly approaches Ibsen and Chekhov, and it would be foolish to think that Neil Simon would be directed primarily from stage directions and the set's floor plan as drawn in the back of the script. Being true to the author's intent does not necessarily mean being true to the original director's and designer's ideas.

Now before I invoke the wrath of creative directors everywhere, let me clarify my position on the subject. I have worked extensively under both conditions. My early years in theater—during the seventies—were as founder and artistic director of Celebration Playhouse, a one-hundred-seat theater with giant aspirations. During the few years of its existence (eventually shuttered due to spiraling orchestra costs, but that's another story altogether), we prided ourselves on experimentation. In addition to such small-scale fare that actually "fit" comfortably in the black-box space—*The Fantasticks; You're a Good Man, Charlie Brown; Butterflies Are Free; Play It Again, Sam; Robber Bridegroom;* and the like, we brazenly adapted shows that really had no business being done in this space. *A Little Night Music, Company, Two Gentlemen of Verona, Gypsy, Lenny,* and *Candide* were all forced into the space with extreme adaptations. And believe it or not, a lot of them actually worked. In fact, we developed a reputation for this sort of challenge. I'll never forget the way we solved the huge banquet table in act 2 of *Night Music* when Mrs. Armfeldt holds her weekend in the country—it lowered down from the ceiling and played suspended above the floor!

At the other extreme, the theater where I currently am the producing director has a very large proscenium stage, a full production staff, a Union orchestra and, while we do not have a fly loft, we can handle large and extensive scenery. We charge a nominal five dollars for adult admission, four dollars for seniors, and children twelve and under are admitted free. It is the mission statement of Plays-in-the-Park (PIP) to re-create as closely as possible the Broadway experience for our audience, many of whom cannot afford the 2004 $100 New York ticket prices.

When we did *A Little Night Music* at PIP, we were able to build the eighteen-foot-tall birch trees out of wood and scrim and track them on in each scene; we created the two period automobiles used during the top of act 2, and our orchestra played the Sondheim score grandly. Our audience got a true taste of what the show felt like on Broadway.

So, if I have worked successfully in both re-creating and reinterpreting shows, why do I have such strong and disparate feelings about the subject? I think it's because in my thirty years producing and directing I have all too often encountered a director who arrogantly refused to research the shows and felt it was his duty and creative mission to do it his own way. This is fine for Nicholas Hytner, who so brilliantly revitalized *Carousel* in 1994 at Lincoln Center, or Sam Mendes, whose extraordinary reshaping of *Cabaret* in 1998 took Broadway by storm, or Susan H. Schulman, who revisited *Sweeney Todd* in 1989 and completely rethought the physical production. These are established theater professionals, working in tandem with the original authors and composers (or members of their estate) and they have all the resources of the New York theater community behind them.

But when a fresh-out-of-college director turns his or her nose up at the original production and feels they bring enough experience to the table to completely reinvent the wheel solely because he or she wants to, I question the motives. Too many directors have told me that they feel I am insulting them by suggesting that they research any and all materials available from the original production. They take it as a personal affront to their creativity. They feel that emulating the Broadway show does not take any invention on their part. I argue that it takes creativity to adapt a show to your cast and technical specifications and still maintain the flavor of the original.

When we did *Kiss Me, Kate*, which is available on DVD, one of the things that struck us about this wonderful video version is the extraordinary talent of the dancers. We attract good dancers (well . . . great female dancers and decent male dancers), but not consistently Broadway caliber. The sets are also outstanding, but far too large a scale for us. So our challenge was to create the flavor of the tour while adapting it to our stage and performers. When our audience watched the show, they came away with the feeling of having seen the intention of the professionally revised *Kiss Me, Kate*.

As another example, in the late eighties we did a production at my theater of a popular show and created it in such a manner as to have the look and feel of the original. When we decided to remount this trivial but popular musical again in the late nineties I interviewed directors whom I felt might bring some new vision to the production. One such candidate told me about a version of *Company* that he had helmed where he set the entire show in a New York subway! That sounded so outlandish that he piqued my interest and I hired him.

The production he delivered for us is still talked about at the theater—fortunately enough years have passed that we laugh about it—as the worst show ever to be done there, and a terrible experience for all those involved. But what bothered me the most was the audience reaction—I received letter after letter about how they felt cheated in not getting to see the show they *expected* to see.

That's it in a nutshell—the audience's expectations. Know your audience, what they want to see, and how they want it to be presented. Those going to see a show off off Broadway or a new show at a college black-box theater will expect something very different than those going to a summer stock house expecting to see *Mame*.

If the theater you are working at is, for whatever reason, not capable of re-creating a show with the flavor of the original, or you or the producer are adventurously wanting to drastically alter a production, then by all means do it—*but* please, don't ignore the roots of the original show. Still do your research, because only after you completely understand the original concept and design can you deconstruct it and intelligently make choices that won't undermine the author's intents. It is both exciting and refreshing to see a new slant on an old production when it is done with taste, creativity, and most important, a respect for the original work. You must do what is right for your theater and your audience, and that's the bottom line.

This whole discussion touches on the legality of copying to the last detail the original production values of a Broadway show, which is not what I am suggesting. I thought it might be both prudent and insightful to talk to a professional about this subject, and so I reached out to an authority, John Prignano, who is the senior vice-president at Music Theatre International, the leasing house for so many of my favorite musicals. John told me that this question is asked of him all the time, but where I find that many directors don't want to even research the original show let alone copy it, he is asked more often than not if a director can indeed replicate the original. John told me that with very few exceptions, an amateur director or choreographer cannot re-create exactly what they might view on a DVD because the original direction and choreography (and set, light, and costume design) is the "intellectual property" of its creator and thus protected under copyright laws. He admits that certain bits of business are intrinsic to the success of the show, like the concept for *Forever Plaid*, so there it is assumed and accepted that every theater group will emulate it. And for some shows, such as Jerome Robbins' choreography for *Fiddler on the Roof*, a detailed choreography manual is included with the standard set of materials (at no additional fee) and should be used for each production. MTI also offers detailed choreography manuals for other shows such as *West Side Story* and *The World Goes Round*; however, the use of the choreography for these shows is optional and can be licensed from MTI for a royalty fee. It's a tricky subject, and one that will continue to be debated as long as there is theater.

5

Preproduction

Having done your research and settled on a stylistic approach to the material, it is time to begin preproduction with your actual staff. You are no longer working in a vacuum. This step involves a series of meetings with everyone from the producer and your designers to your stage manager (SM).

Communication is the key. All too often tech week approaches and I find that a prop isn't quite right, or the door on the set that I thought opened out actually opens in. Communication and production meetings can avert so many of these annoyances. One thing is for certain—regardless of what type of meeting you are attending, take copious notes. Don't leave anything to memory.

Your first meeting would be with the producer or board of directors. You would have met with him (or her or them) prior to the interview to discuss the job, but now that you have the position and have done your homework, you will want to sit down and talk nuts and bolts. Here are a number of topics worth discussing:

- What is the theater's policy on casting? Is the final say up to the director (in tandem with the choreographer and musical director, if applicable) or is the producer/board involved in the casting decisions? Is there—heaven forbid—a "casting committee"? Once this is determined, you'll want to plan the dates for the auditions.

- What sort of rehearsal schedule will you be able to set up? Is the theater available for rehearsals or will there be an alternate space? In the case of a high school or even college assignment, will the stage be yours for the whole rehearsal period—allowing the stage manager to tape out the floor plan and for you to leave furniture, and so forth, in place—or will there be other events happening that will disrupt the flow and force the rehearsal setup to be more temporary? Will rehearsal props be made available to you or is it a catch-as-catch-can situation, using things found lying about?

- In the case of a musical, you'll want to know the size of the orchestra and when you will have them for rehearsals. Even more important, will there be a rehearsal pianist at every rehearsal or will you be working from a tape made by the musical director or, worse, the CD of the original cast? Do your best to avoid the latter—they barely resemble the actual score. If you will be working from a cassette—or if the theater is so equipped, a minidisc—then you'll want to make one of your next meetings a discussion with the musical director to figure out when he or she can record this tape for you.

As a side note—and once again this attests to the visionaries at Music Theater International—when you license a musical from MTI you can rent from them something called a RehearScore, which is a complete rendition of the piano-conductor score on CD-ROM sequenced by a top Broadway pianist. Each disk includes a player that works on both Windows and Mac computers, and includes scene change, dance music, and underscoring! Bravo!

- You'll want to discuss budget with the producer. It will be helpful for you to know, even if you are not directly concerned with expenditures, the type of monetary allocations made for costuming, scenery, props, lighting equipment rentals, and special effects, if applicable. It will give you an idea of how grandiose you can be in planning the scope of the show—whether you can envision intelligent lighting fixtures that move with the actors or a hydraulic lift to raise Sweeney out of the stage floor or lower the Wicked Witch when she melts. You are well aware of what types of effects the show calls for, having done all that research! In fact, if you envision such theatrical magic, this would be the time and place to get the yea or nay from the producer. Of course, if the theater more or less expects you to act as producer and oversee how each department spends the budget, then this subject might be the very first one you'll want to discuss with the powers that be. Unfortunately, this adds an unwanted burden to your responsibilities and forces you to be involved in areas outside the artistic. If you find yourself in this position you'll want to meet with your designers ASAP to go over the budget.

- What is your responsibility to the show once it opens . . . are you finished after opening night or expected to check up on the show during the run?
- Finally, you'll want to question the producer for any helpful hints that have worked in the past in making a successful production at their particular theater. You're fishing for inside bits and pieces that pleased them as well as the things that rankled them. It would be very nice to learn from prior director's mistakes!

Once you've met successfully with the producing branch of the theater, you'll want to have a production meeting with the set designer, costume designer, lighting designer (LD), prop master or mistress, stage manager, any assistants, and, if applicable, the choreographer and the musical director.

Actually, you'll want to have a series of meetings, perhaps one every two weeks or so until the show has opened. These will be crucial to the successful integration of all the various disciplines. More than likely the producer will want to be present—if he or she is at all "hands-on"—and, thus, scheduling can be a bear. Utilize your stage manager to coordinate, and have smaller meetings with a select few if need be. Just make sure the SM documents every meeting, in writing, and that copies are distributed to all involved. Again, leave nothing to memory.

In your initial meeting with your design staff, you'll want to share both your concept and your research. You might suggest, in keeping with my *Jekyll and Hyde* example, that the costumer follow up on some of the Web pages you discovered, and that the set designer watch the video for ideas, especially if there are design elements you wish to utilize in your blocking. And above all, let them know how *you* envision the show. Instill in them an enthusiasm for the way you intend to make the show work—artistically, technically, and creatively.

Set a schedule for the following deadlines from the set designer and costumer: (1) when initial designs are due from both designers; (2) when an actual model will be available from the set designer; (3) when work will begin; and (4) when you will actually have things to work with. The producer will have input in this, but certainly you want to be very specific about tech week. This is especially crucial if you won't be able to rehearse on the set prior. Many theaters begin work on the set right away, and you'll enjoy working on sections of it as soon as you start blocking. Other theaters, particularly summer-stock houses, may not load in a set until tech.

If you're lucky, you can be adding props and utilizing the set as you go along, but not so in every venue. If you won't get everything until tech, you'll need to request that things be prioritized. If you have five rehearsals to tech the show, you might request that the set be in place and operable, even if not totally painted and dressed, by the first tech rehearsal. You might also ask that all hand props be available at this time as well. The second rehearsal might be a cue to cue to rough in the lights, while the third one would have the costumes added. The final two would be full dress rehearsals with everything ready.

All of this should be discussed at the first or second meeting, and a calendar prepared by the stage manager should be distributed. This may all seem obvious, but depending on the theater and the experience of the staff, this sort of regimentation might not be what they are used to. Having everything planned out and documented can avoid countless headaches (and disappointments) later on.

The lighting designer, of course, can't produce anything preproduction, but you'll want to have lengthy discussions on concept and cues, especially if your blocking will directly impact the lighting and vice versa. Discuss "specials"; evening and daytime scenes; special effects; the use of follow spots, if applicable; and practical lighting (lighting instruments such as table lamps, neon signs, chandeliers—which often dictate the look of the stage lighting itself). The LD would, of course, sit in on any number of rehearsals to make notes and plan the design. Directorial ideas can be discussed at this time.

Two weeks or so before I know the lighting designer will be hanging the plot, I prepare a written printout of every scene and what lighting demands I foresee. We review the notes together at a production meeting or rehearsal. It might be as simple as:

ACT ONE
Scene 3
On the London Streets, outside Jekyll's study.
In this scene I'd like to have a practical old English street-lamp casting a glow on the door to the study. The cyc might be a deep blue.

Or as complicated as:

ACT TWO
Scene 6
In this scene the actor playing Jekyll and Hyde sings the duet with himself. For everything he sings as Jekyll, please have the lights come from stage right and above right, and gel them warm. When he is Hyde, use the opposite side of the stage and gel them red. Additionally, the beakers and other lab equipment should glow from below—can we make a Plexiglas counter top with lights inside? Use the footlights in this scene as well—maybe just with Hyde?

Obviously this is a situation where (a) the director has the final say on all aspects of the production and (b) the director has a good working relationship with the designer, who respects and even asks for his input. There might be instances where each designer works in a vacuum and does precisely what he pleases, but in my humble opinion, the chances of such a show having a cohesive, uniform concept are not very good.

Even if everyone were working on their own, communication would be imperative. I strongly suggest that all the designers share their ideas with all involved. At the first meeting, you might come prepared with an initial prop list, or at the very least, use the one sometimes included in the back of a play script (musicals rarely provide prop lists, but straight plays and comedies often do). If it is inappropriate at the first meeting to discuss props, ask your SM to prepare a list for the next meeting, review it beforehand, and then make it a topic of discussion. If you are going to get rehearsal props, this would be the time to ask for those essential props that impact on the actors.

As a side note, and again this may be obvious, email now provides a most effective method of communication. Notes of every meeting can be typed up in Word documents, formatted professionally into tables, and emailed with the click of a mouse to everyone—those who attended the meeting and those absent. It creates an electronic paper trail that you can go back to when questions arise. When the carpenters build a platform eight feet high that should have been only six feet, you can go back to your notes, complete with a date stamp, and show them the error.

As soon as I am given the names (and email addresses) of my production staff I create a group mailing list so that I can reach everyone easily. I'll do the same with the actors, once cast. I once told a stage manager that I could *not* rehire him until he got himself an email address. I told him Hotmail could solve his problem with a free account, and once he signed up, he found how invaluable the technology was: for rehearsal schedules and subsequent changes, for messages to the staff, to distribute notes from the director to the cast, and so on.

Your meetings, in the case of a musical, with the choreographer and musical director will most likely take place separately from the meetings with the design crew, although the choreographer in particular will want to be at those meetings as well. Sometimes even more than the director, the choreographer needs to know the footprint of a set piece to know how much dancing space there is, where the drops will play, and if there are any various rises or rakes in or on the stage. Dances, and dancers, need space not only left and right but upstage and downstage, and it is quite important for the set designer and the choreographer to be on the same page in order to avoid unwanted surprises the first time the dancers work on the set. Dances will be stilted if they are attempted on too cramped a stage, and without depth, they will be primarily linear, which tends to look like a dance recital.

Your meetings with these two collaborators will be ongoing; in fact, once the rehearsal process begins, you'll be inseparable. While I will go into more detail on the subject in a subsequent chapter, there seems to be two ways of collaborating with a chore-ographer. In one scenario, you really do everything more or less together. My partner at PIP will work on a number, and then show it to me and we'll dissect it. When she stages it, I'll be there with my support. I'll often stage the solo songs, and then call her in to give them crispness, focus, and life. A true collaboration.

There are, however, directors and choreographers who work independently. They may even work in different spaces on the same evening, and only during the first run-through does one see what the other has created. This would not work for me, but if you are in the situation where this is what is expected, there will undoubtedly have to be a lot of meetings to discuss how a dance number will evolve out of the blocking, which ensemble members will be involved, and how the number will be inte-grated into the show. Otherwise there will be no cohesive flow to the production.

The relationship with the musical director is slightly different. More often than not the musical director will teach the music to the cast on his own. Because the music is a given—unlike the block-ing or choreography—his work is more instructional. All three col-laborators need to be on the same page when it comes to any potential cuts made to the music, especially the dance music. Many of the older musicals had very long dance breaks—some even used ballet (*Oklahoma,* for example) and it is the shrewd choreographer who knows that less is more. It is far better to use 32 measures of exciting, well-executed dance combinations than to see 120 bars of boring or repetitive movement. What is to be cut, and how the remaining measures will fit together, is something to be done prior to the first rehearsal in your production meetings. A reminder: you will need to get permission from the licensing company (MTI, Samuel French, Tams-Witmark, etc.) before you make any cuts or alterations to the music, book, or lyrics.

As with the lighting designer, you will want to also meet fre-quently with the sound designer. Of special importance is the use of sound effects. The designer will need to know specifically what sounds you will need, and how they are utilized within the pro-duction. If body microphones or other sound enforcement is to be used, the sound designer will need to sit in on rehearsals prior to tech week to determine the type of equipment to be used and its placement.

In closing, if at all possible, try to meet with the designers at least once a week prior to rehearsals for as many weeks as you can, and then more often during the actual rehearsal period. You will want to meet with your stage manager daily, even if via email, as well as your choreographer and musical director if you're working on a musical.

6

Casting

I feel very strongly that if you cast your show properly, your job will be cut in half. The right actors in the right roles can make a show, and you will not be burdened with acting lessons or trying to adapt a character to the actor. Therefore, it behooves the director to treat the audition process very seriously and arrive at a method of casting that is comfortable, thorough, and not hurried.

If this is a nonmusical and non-Equity production, then you most likely can handle everything in two sessions—two evenings or two weekend days, whichever works out. One day for the initial open call and another for callbacks. If it is an Equity production you might need an additional day for the Equity open call, another for the non-Equity call and a third for callbacks. A musical can take as many as five or six days, and includes open calls plus callbacks that involve readings, dance combinations, singing specific passages, and pairing people up.

Let me interject here a word about casting committees. You might find yourself in a situation in which there is a committee appointed to make the casting decisions. While this doesn't happen often, some community theaters do use this practice. I am not in favor of this method for a number of reasons, the chief being that it is unlikely (if not impossible) for people outside of the production to share the artistic vision of the director (and, in the case of a musical, the choreographer and musical director) and then make an appropriate decision. All too frequently a committee member may have a hidden agenda and can influence casting for wrong reasons. As obnoxious as it may sound, the theater is not a democracy. The director needs to be in charge artistically, and in the case of casting committees, the cliché "too many cooks" truly applies.

Let's start with a non-Equity call for a straight play. Let us use, as an example, *Lend Me a Tenor*, an eight-character comedy. I have scheduled two days for auditions, a Monday and a Tuesday night. Monday is the open call; Tuesday the callback. The casting notice has gone out—to all the local newspapers. Additionally, the blurb is posted online on the theater's website, and flyers have been distributed to schools, libraries, and other local theaters. The notice reads (and I have taken some liberties with the character breakdowns):

> *Open casting has been announced for The Starstruck Theater's pro-duction of Ken Ludwig's classic farce* Lend Me a Tenor, *playing for two weekends, Thursday, Friday, and Saturday evenings, April 12 through 21, with a matinee each Sunday.*
>
> *The auditions will be held at the theater (see our website or call the theater for directions). The open call for all roles will be Monday, March 1, at 7:30 and the callback will be on Tuesday, March 2, at 7:30. The open call is first come, first served.*
>
> *The cast breakdown is as follows:*
>
> *MAX—a nervous young man in his late twenties*
> *MAGGIE—his pretty girlfriend, in her twenties*
> *SAUNDERS—general manager of the Opera Company, fifties, highly excitable, apt to bellow*
> *TITO—world-famous tenor, in his thirties to early forties, tall and imposing, a ladies' man*
> *MARIA—mid-thirties, Tito's long-suffering wife*
> *BELLHOP—early twenties, eager to please*
> *DIANA—mid-thirties, a diva in the opera company*
> *JULIA—sixties, chairwoman of the Opera Guild, dotty*
>
> *Come to the open call with a two- to three-minute comic monologue prepared. The characters of Max and Tito ideally should be able to sing well, and so if you are auditioning for either of those roles, pre-pare sixteen measures of an operatic passage to sing a capella.*
>
> *Please bring a photo and resume.*
>
> *For further information, call (785) 876-0098.*

I would have my stage manager prepare audition forms that would ask for name, address, home phone, cell phone, email address, height, age range (some people won't put an age, but will fill in an age range), and a section for conflicts, which is most important when making up the rehearsal schedule. If I know I am going to rehearse Monday through Thursday evenings and Sunday afternoons, I will note that on the audition sheet so that those auditioning can fill in potential conflicts. The audition form might also have a space (or the back) for a resume if they don't have one prepared. At callbacks I will further explain that since the schedule is not set in stone it can be adapted to conflicts. Therefore if anyone needs to revisit their sheet to be more accurate, they should do so.

When people arrive at the audition—often an hour earlier—I will have the stage manager take names and hand out the forms, numbering them in the order people arrive. The SM can staple or paper-clip their photos and resumes to the audition form. When the time to begin approaches, I will have them come into the theater one at a time, hand me their form, and perform their monologue. At that point I will make some notes as to my impressions, and either thank them for coming or ask them to come back the next night for a callback. I'll then note the role(s) for which I have them in mind. I often keep a digital camera on hand just in case they don't have a photo.

I have found that the initial open calls should be private—in fact, Equity demands it. I will, however, usually have the callbacks held as a group, for a number of reasons. I feel that those auditioning should see the competition. In situations where everyone knows virtually everyone else—as with long-standing community theaters—it is good for everyone to see for himself or herself why I went in the direction I went. Of course some actors will never see past their own audition, but there's nothing to be done about that. Furthermore, in the case of a musical, it is unrealistic to teach a dance combination or a vocal section individually; and if there is a big turnout you'll want to watch the dancers three, four, or even five or six at a time. Last, I like to see how actors look next to each other. Is the girl I have in mind for the lead towering above the leading man? Does the potential ensemble look right together? You can't tell unless all the potentials are in the same room at the same time.

I will often videotape the callbacks as well (but only if the show is non-Equity, since Equity forbids this) and I have occasionally changed my mind after studying the video a day later. An Equity callback is trickier. The Equity rulebook states: *Performers shall be auditioned individually and shall not be called in groups unless necessary for physical screening, movement, and/or vocal blending.* This means that you can still teach the dance combination en masse but will have to do your readings in private.

There are a number of ways of announcing who is to be called back: you can tell them right away after their open call; you can make phone calls the next morning; you can post it on the Internet or, in the case of a high school or college, on the drama or music room door or callboard. It all depends on the particular theater and the time frame involved. If there is a day or two between the open call and the callbacks you have more options.

Back to *Lend Me a Tenor*. Once the open call is finished, you'll want to review all the material you have prepared for the callback. Using the play script, I find a cutting from monologues or two-to-three-people scenes that I want to use for the readings. I will often retype them so that they are more clearly read by the actors. Sometimes I will combine bits and pieces of a few different monologues spoken by the same character or if he or she has only a few scattered lines to make a more interesting reading. I have also been known to rewrite lines slightly to eliminate superfluous characters who might have an occasional line here and there.

What you are trying to do is create a monologue or a dialogue that is long enough to give you an idea of what the actor can do, but not too long—especially if you are reading a lot of people for the same role. I have found that half to three-quarters of a page works nicely for a monologue; two pages for a multicharacter scene.

Depending on the character, you will need to decide if you want to hear the actor alone doing a monologue from the show (compiled, or otherwise) or if you want two characters to read together. To make more sense of this, let's look again at *Lend Me a Tenor*. This is a show where lightning-fast dialogue between characters is key to its success, so in my opinion I'd like to read characters together—to see how they play off each other and to see how they look together. I'd find a scene between Max and Maggie, the young lovers. Then I'd find another scene between Tito and Maria, the husband and wife. There are a few good scenes with Julia and Saunders, and with Tito and Diana. If you have a number of them at the ready, you can mix and match as need be.

What do you do if you are forced into individual callbacks? Well, then, you'll have to use your stage manager as a reader; or better yet, if you have an actor friend you can rely on, use him—he might give the actor auditioning more input to work with. Unless you are under Equity rules, take all the time you need to make the right decisions. Consider experience, conflicts, first impressions and, of course, their readings and their look.

The question often comes up when you've previously worked with certain actors—do you go with someone you know or try someone new? It's a difficult question and opinions will vary—but if there are two people up for a role and one is decidedly the better choice, then I would always go with the better choice. But if two actors are really quite equal and you know one of them, I am always more comfortable with the actor I know—provided, of course, they truly are right for the part and you get along. There will be plenty of actors who will need your coaching and individual hand-holding—if you can cast a few actors who already know your style and what to expect, the whole process will go that much more smoothly. Theater is, after all, a business, and you need to do whatever you need to do to make the final outcome the best it can be.

What about precasting, you ask? Again, my opinion, but I feel that as long as you make it perfectly clear up front—from the casting blurb to the listing on your website to any postings on the Internet—that a certain role is already cast, then it is an acceptable practice. What is decidedly unfair is to not announce that certain roles have been cast and allow, even encourage, people to audition for them. This is unconscionable.

Casting musicals is a larger process. In anticipation of a greater turnout, you might schedule two open calls, perhaps a Friday evening and a Saturday afternoon, offering optimal opportunities for people to attend. Your callbacks might also span two sessions. At the open call I normally ask for the best sixteen bars (measures) of a show tune (pop songs are rarely appropriate for a musical audition unless the show is *Rent*, *Tommy*, or *Little Shop of Horrors*) and for the actors to bring their own sheet music, in the proper key, marked for the accompanist. I do not encourage singing a capella, nor to a tape. It just doesn't show off the performer in the best light—it becomes about getting the tape deck plugged or cued up, or trying to find a key to sing a capella. I'd rather hear "God Bless America" accompanied on the piano than "Tomorrow" sung without. I ask for pictures and resumes as well—that part of the process is the same as a straight play.

At the open call you are listening to the actor's voice and typing them physically—quickly deciding if they could possibly fill a role. It is at the callback that you will see a dance combination, hear them read from the script and possibly sing a section of a song from the show—including the most difficult "money note(s)"—usually the ending. It might be prudent to note that some theaters, where turnouts are limited, could choose to hold the open call and callbacks all on the same evening. You might have a callback form printed with information on which you can quickly check off potential role(s), if they need tap or jazz shoes, or a specific time to come to callbacks and you can then hand these out after they sing. You might even print up a sheet to hand out to those who don't receive a callback, explaining that there wasn't anything for them this show (or season) but to please come back and audition again. This is much more pleasant than simply saying "thank you" and sending them on their way.   •

Sometimes directors even prefer to give out the sides (the monologues or dialogues from the show that the actor will audition with at the callback) in advance, or post them on the Internet. It's a personal preference—some directors want to hear a cold reading while others like to hear what the actor has done with the piece given time to rehearse it.

There are pros and cons to both methods. A cold reading can show whether the actor can think on his feet—his ability to create on the spot. A practiced audition will show what he is capable of doing on his own. In either case, it is often helpful to throw a different interpretation at the actor after his initial reading for you—just to see if he can adapt, take direction, and has versatility.

Whether you have one night to hold your callbacks or two or more, you'll want to have a game plan that utilizes your (and the actor's) time well. Many actors will be more concerned over the dance and singing auditions than they are over the readings; thus it is sometimes a good idea to hold those first. Dancers are often panicked over the vocals, and nondancers might dread the dance combination. Getting these done first also might provide an opportunity to let some people go home—a "first-cut," if you will.

If an actor or actress has a gorgeous voice and looks perfect but just can't dance at all, it would probably be wrong to cast him as Tulsa in *Gypsy* or her as Lottie in *Mack and Mabel*. You might keep these people in mind for another role or the singing ensemble, but you probably won't need to hear them read if there isn't a supporting or principal role for them. I will add, however, that some theaters and directors prefer to give everyone a chance at all three—dancing, singing, and reading—regardless, especially if there isn't a large turnout or this is a high school or college situation and because, of course, there might be a triple threat waiting to audition (triple threat meaning a wonderful dancer, singer, and actor). If there is no one better, however, you just might need to utilize an awkward Tulsa—although that surely would defeat the purpose of his song. Admittedly Tulsa might be a bad example. Still, there are other dancing roles where you might be able to get away with a nondancer if you surround him (or her) with a strong dancing ensemble. Community theater, unfortunately, can be fraught with compromise.

Here's a possible callback scenario for a big old musical. You'll want to teach everything right away—meaning any choreography and any specific songs. If you can arrange for two keyboard players—perhaps the musical director and the rehearsal pianist (if you have a separate rehearsal pianist)—then you can take one group into a separate room while another on stage learns something else.

I try to schedule the principals and larger supporting roles on one day, and the ensemble on another day. In this hypothetical situation, imagine day one with three leading male roles to cast and four leading females. Two of the male roles don't require extraordinary voices so they can both learn a section from the same song. The other two men have strong vocal demands so they must each learn a single selection. That's three musical selections for the men. Three of the women are soprano roles; they can share the same piece of music. The fourth girl is a belter—she'll need her own. That's two more pieces. If you can divide the women into two rooms, you can probably teach the music in a half hour, assuming each selection is between sixteen and thirty-two bars. In each case, you have selected a section of the song that requires the performers to hit the high note, or the sustained note, or in some way shows that they can put this particular song across to the audience.

If feasible, and if your choreographer is clever, you might be able to combine the dance combinations as well. Two of the women have to tap, so you prepare a thirty-two-bar tap combination for them. But the rest of the dancing demands are more or less "theater-dance-generic" and so you come up with a combination that starts off easy, and then half-way through turns more difficult. This might take another half hour to teach. All the women and the men learn the first half and then the nondancers drop out and the others continue through the second half. If you were ever so lucky as to find a guy who says—"hey, I can do that"—then he also continues through the whole combination. Every once in a while you do find men who have dance training and can execute the more challenging parts of the routine.

Once everything is learned, it might be best to audition the dance first so everyone can relax a bit. By bringing five performers up at a time, and making them dance the combination twice, you can get through it quickly. Have them audition two downstage, three upstage, set up like bowling pins, and for the second go-around, they can change lines. Once this is done and you've made copious notes (I use a grading system of 1 to 4, with 4 the best), you can move on to the singing. Review en masse at the piano first, then have them sing individually, grading as you go. I ask them to not only sing the song to their best ability, quality-wise, but also to act the song—in other words, to "sell it."

With this out of the way, everyone can relax a bit. You might find that you can make a first cut, letting some go home. If that's the case, I often make a speech along these lines: "The fact that you are being eliminated now does not mean you will not be cast in the show—it merely means we have seen all we need to see for certain roles." I then thank them and give them info on when and how the cast will be announced.

Whether you've made a first cut or not, it is time for the readings. If you haven't chosen to post the sides sooner, you can give them out now. Give them a few minutes to absorb the material, and then call them up individually or in pairs, mixing and matching to your heart's content, always making notes and grading the readings.

If you are using a note pad, write clearly. If you use a laptop, create a table in Excel or Word with various columns: name, audition number, dance, voice, look, reading, general impression, notes, role, and so forth. You can then easily fill in your comments.

If you do it in Excel, you can sort the data in various ways to help when you go home or meet with your collaborators to actually cast the show. By having info in a database, you can quickly sort the audition info based on your "grades" for singing, dancing, or on general impression. You can group actors according to characters for comparison. You might even be able to judge conflicts with rehearsals if you previously entered that info into the database.

Some theaters make their choices the same night, and your notes will serve as a refresher. If time permits, it is often a nice gesture to ask if anyone would like to read for something that they haven't had the opportunity to do. They might see themselves in a different role than you do. You never know, this might produce some revelations.

Before I let everyone go home, I usually end with something along these lines: "You have been called back tonight because you are all *A* players. If this were Broadway, our ensemble and supporting roles would be made up of actors of your caliber. We're going to choose our leads from this group, but we also hope that you will allow us to consider you for smaller roles as well, which would be wonderful for our show. If, however, you only want a leading role, please mention that to our stage manager. There will, I promise, be no repercussions. We'd rather your honesty now than to cast you only to have you turn the role down. In any case, thank you for this long evening and you'll hear from us within a few days . . . ."

Depending on the size of your turnout, you might phone those actors who are cast, or, if it isn't too overwhelming, it's nice to call or email everyone whether they are cast or not, thanking those turned down and encouraging them to come back again for another show. It is often wise to have a second and even a third choice in mind for each role, especially in those areas where there are a lot of competitive theaters. Actors will sometimes turn down roles for no apparent reason; or perhaps they have auditioned for a few shows in the same time period and are holding off until they see what possible roles they can choose from—good for them, bad for the directors. You might have everything planned perfectly with an ideal cast only to find that two actors turn you down when you call. This can have a domino effect on the entire process because you might now wish to bump up someone else and move others around, so be prepared. Have a contingency plan. And call the most important roles—or those you suspect might be an issue—first.

7

Working with the Designers

You've had your initial production meetings with the various designers. Now it is the time to get serious. Much of this chapter is devoted to working with the set designer, simply because it is this collaboration that most impacts your blocking and staging of the show, and you need to know the ins and outs of the set design in advance so you can really do your job effectively. Second in importance would be the costumer, and last, the lighting designer, whose work you won't really get to judge until tech week. If the props are the least bit complicated, you meet with your propster(s), too, as rehearsals progress.

It is always insightful in dealing with your collaborators if you have at one time tackled each of their disciplines. I have worked as a set designer often, as a lighting designer occasionally, and as a costumer never, but my partner has been a costumer. Together we can speak their languages and communicate ideas effectively. If you've never designed, I'm not suggesting you suddenly change careers, but it would be helpful to read up on what it takes to work in these areas.

Sets

A nonmusical will often have a single set design—a room or two, a park bench, whatever. If the designer provides you with a scale model of the design, a white model—which means it hasn't yet been painted—prior to your blocking, then you can think everything through. I have known directors who have taken chess pieces to represent actors and actually blocked the show on the model, later transcribing their ideas into the script.

Among what would be important in a one-set show would be where the doors and windows are, if it is an interior; which way they open (in or out); the placement of the furniture, the height of the ceiling if applicable, and so on. This isn't to say you can't have input—you certainly can—but this is where diplomacy comes into play. Theater is a world of egos—both insecure ones and hugely confident ones—and your people skills should be finely honed to avoid clashes. The key to this is to convey your needs as early in the process as possible. It would not be altogether fair to take a look at a finished set model and tell the designer that that the door he created should actually be a double-sized archway—he will be understandably annoyed.

Based on all your research—see, I told you it was important—you should have a very good idea of what the specific staging needs are, and it is your responsibility to tell the designer that there are certain necessities for the staging. This most likely wouldn't dictate the type of wallpaper or window treatments needed, but if there needs to be an escape off the back of the stairs or a practical window on the second floor, make sure you and the designer are in agreement.

Communication becomes even more crucial when dealing with a multiset play and, above all, when dealing with a musical. A director has to know how the set designer intends for the sets to come on- and off-stage, how they join together, and where they play on stage. You cannot very well plan your stage movement until you have the answers to these questions. When I am the set designer at my theater I get many phone calls from the director during the week or so that they are planning their blocking. Can the second level of the library hold six people? Should I have actors plan on rolling out that set piece or will stagehands (ideally dressed in black) move the piece? Does the revolving platform circle to the left or to the right? The questions don't stop—and believe me, I more than appreciate them. The more communication at the beginning, the fewer disasters during tech. Plus, with each question I am forced to reevaluate my choices and to make sure I like everything I've done. A good set designer should never feel put upon by a director who wants to know the set design intimately.

If you can convince the set designer to leave the model with you for an evening or even a few nights, it is helpful to sit and study the model, moving it around your floor plan if you have one, looking at it from an actor's point of view, the director's point of view, and the audience's point of view. I can't stress strongly enough how a thorough understanding of the set and how it is to be used can make or break your tech week, especially in a musical, where there may be multiple sets and you'll want a smooth transition between set changes and enough space for choreography. You'll also want to utilize the set as much as possible. When I directed *Follies* there was a large set of steps center stage. If I hadn't had a firm grasp of their size and scope before rehearsals I might have underutilized them, resulting in the audience's wondering why they were even there.

For my money, there is nothing more intolerable, and unforgivable, than long set changes. This can be prevalent in high school shows—the lights sort of fade to black while we wait an excruciatingly long time for the crew to get one set off and the other on. Avoiding this is as much the director's job—in coordination with the designer—as is directing the actors and staging the movement. Careful planning and preproduction work can, on the other hand, present enlightened methods of making set changes flow quickly and smoothly—even interestingly! If they are considered as choreographed sections, they can be a fascinating part of a play or musical. One method that works well for me is to have cast members change scenery in partial light, called avista. If the techies get the sets in the proper positions in the wings, then actors, in character or not, can do the rest of the work, moving the pieces in place. The lighting designer might choose to glow the stage in a blue wash rather than going to black so the audience can actually see the shift happening. If it is done with flair by actors in costume and timed to the scene change music, it can actually be an effective element of the show.

In those rare instances in a straight play where there are multiple sets that are not changed during intermission, you might want to consider adding sound or music to help the scene change work more smoothly. If you use original music, there are no copyright issues; use pop songs at your own risk.

As a side note, background music can breathe life into a drama or comedy even if there wasn't any music originally connected with the show. In a production of *Arsenic and Old Lace*, I used underscoring to embellish the mood in two or three scenes where the evil brother was up to some mayhem. Music being played through a jukebox or an on-stage radio has been written in to a number of shows (*Hot L Baltimore*, for example) and might work with many others. To quote a line from *Chicago*, "it's all showbiz, kid"; thus, anything you can do to make the evening more theatrical is a good thing.

Costumes

The collaboration with the costume designer, while not as obvious as that of the set designer, is equally important. There are two aspects of the costume design that the director should take an interest in. The first is, of course, the accuracy, authenticity, creativity, and artistry of the costumes. The second is the functionality of the costumes within the play or musical.

You might assume that if you hired a respected and talented designer this would all be taken care of perfectly. But people's visions often vary, so you need to make sure that you and the designer are on the same wavelength. This can only be accomplished by a number of meetings, and through—here's that word again—research. Whenever you can show the designer a picture of what you mean, well, it's worth a thousand words.

There are wonderful costume designers working on all levels of theater whom you can trust to deliver a stunning show. There are also well meaning but less-talented designers who need guidance, and then there are volunteers (for example, mothers) who sew—which is what you might expect at a high school. Depending on the designer, your involvement can be minimal or highly collaborative.

When it comes to costumes, there are a number of ways to go. The costumes can be rented in part or entirely from a costume rental house. I have worked on shows where the rental house actually supplies every costume, pulled by someone at the rental house, which has worked out quite well. I have also worked on shows where only a portion of the costumes were rented and the designer was very, very specific with the costume shop, asking that photos of these costumes be emailed for approval.

The next option is to pull costumes from the theater's stock—assuming they have some—and alter and refurbish as need be. I have worked at high schools that have amassed quite a collection over the years, and colleges often have warehouses full. Depending on the period, clothing can also be bought at thrift shops for some shows.

The third option, which is out of reach for many theaters, is to build the costumes from scratch. This requires a fabulous designer, a staff of stitchers and drapers, a shop, and a hefty budget. Costumers have worked out of their homes when a shop is not available. Experience has shown that most theaters use a combination of all three methods, but regardless, as director, you'll want to approve the costumes or, at the very least, have some input.

The director's second concern in the process has to do with the functionality of the costuming. The director and the choreographer need to make sure that the costumes allow for the type of movement or dancing required by the script and concept. If the designer is not aware of how you are staging the show, the costumes might be inappropriate to the requirements. For example, high kicks would be all but impossible in a tight skirt. There may be certain comic shtick (*A Funny Thing . . . Forum*) or special effects that involve the costumes. As the director, it is up to you to relay this information to your designer. Of course, I am assuming that the designer (in fact, all your design staff) has carefully read the play, but I have found this simple act occasionally neglected. Insist on it—the script gives a wealth of information as to the season, the locale, and the time period, as well as what specialty items might be required.

There are a number of points during the rehearsal period at which you might want to check up on the progress of the costumes. The first is at the onset, when the costumer has prepared the designs and shows you either sketches, photos, or pictures from a catalog. Here you can at least know the direction the designer is headed, but by no means should this be the only time you get involved. Remember to keep the costumer informed of any nuances added during the rehearsal period; for example, "Tito will need a pocket and a handkerchief," or "It looks like there will be a quick change here—the jacket needs to be rigged accordingly."

The next time might be when the costumer is holding fittings. At this point the rentals have arrived or costumes have been pulled and refurbished and it is time to try them on the actors. This is a good time to get a feel for how things will look on the actors, and, like it or not, get the actor's opinions as well. This is not to say you won't pop into the costume shop on occasion to see the progress or request a peek at the costumes during the scheduled production meetings, but the fittings are your first opportunity to see them on a human being.

Right before you actually begin dress rehearsals, a standard procedure is to hold a costume parade. I usually insist on this on the high school level. A costume parade is time set aside for you and the other designers to see each costume on each actor, usually lined up on the apron of the stage. You might go scene by scene, bringing out everyone from leads to ensemble and looking at how the costumes gel next to each other. Once they have been dissected, give everyone time to change and bring out the next scene with the next look. It's a great way to get a feeling for the big picture. What will certainly stand out is where you might wish to accessorize—add jewelry, hats, scarves, gloves. It's the little details that separate the pros from the amateurs and that transform costumes from ordinary to extraordinary.

Of course, you can, and should, continue to study and improve on the costumes right through the dress-rehearsal period. Needless to say, but I'll say it anyway, as with all your staff, treat the costumer with respect and kindness, even if you feel she has goofed somewhere along the line. It is common courtesy, plus it'll go a long way toward getting your ideas implemented.

The theater world as a community is a small one, and your reputation will quickly spread. This is a good place in the book to mention that you will be more apt to be hired if your reputation is one of kindness and compassion as well as creativity.

Lighting

On to the lighting designer. As I have stated earlier, you won't get to see the lighting designer's work until you are actually into tech week, which makes production meetings and communication all the more important. Convey your ideas as best you can and as soon as possible to the LD, and continue to keep the designer in the loop as things develop during your rehearsals. You should be concerned with, among many things: the time of day the scenes take place, the atmospheric conditions (sunlight, cloudy, rain, etc.), whether the scene is interior or exterior, the light source (sun, fluorescent, table lamps, moonlight), and whether there are "practicals," such as chandeliers, candles, neon signs, or moon or sun boxes.[1]

Atmosphere should be one of the lighting designer's areas of expertise, and your input here might be appreciated. Even such simple words as *bright, cheery, spooky,* or *depressing* can help the LD know which tools to bring out from his or her bag of tricks. By using templates known as gobos, breakups, or patterns, a number of moods or other effects can be created. For an idea of what gobos are and what they can do, visit Rosco's gobo Website at www.rosco-ca.com/products/patterns/. Rosco is by no means the only company, and a search of gobos/patterns/templates will take you to other manufacturers.

Fog machines and hazers are also part of an LD's domain, and can be used to great advantage. A fog machine would be used when you want the audience to actually see the smoke, while a hazer has a different purpose. A hazer puts tiny beads of moisture into the area, creating a haze that picks up the beams of light from a lighting instrument. If you've ever been to a rock concert you'll know the look. Note that the minute a fog machine starts to pour its product out onto the stage a number of people will cough—it's almost Pavlovian. As the director, don't let it bother you. The coughing will soon subside as the audience realizes they are not at risk.

Here's an example—you want the look of a London street at night in a scene from *Jekyll and Hyde*. First, you would buy or rent a streetlamp and make it practical, meaning it would actually light up on stage. Next you would have the LD focus a strong beam of light to shine down as if emanating from the streetlamp, forming a pool of light just left or right of the streetlamp's base. Using strip lights or other specials, you can create a deep blue wash over the stage. Use a moon box cut to represent a full moon and hang it behind the London backdrop and glow it slightly. Then flood the stage with the haze from your hazer, creating not only London's fog but also defining and highlighting the beam of light from the streetlamp. To complete the picture, use a few breakups from the front of the house lighting position to create some eerie shadows. Voila! We're ready for Hyde to strike.

---

1 A moon or sun box is a wooden box (similar to a shadow box) for framing items. The front has a crescent moon or a full circle cut out of it and the back wall contains light bulbs. When the box is suspended from a drop or scrim, the moon or sun appears to be glowing in the distance.

You also need to let the designer know if there are specialties such as a disco light sequence, lightning and thunder, water from a river or a lake shimmering on the scenery. The possibilites are endless, hindered only by the theater's resources and your own creativity. But I urge you to explore any and all effects early on in the process, because, again, the details are what make a production unique.

You might ask, shouldn't the lighting designer know all this? And I would be forced to answer, yes, he or she should. But in the real world, unless you are directing at a regional theater or a college, or unless you just happen to luck out, the person assigned to be your lighting designer might not have the experience, expertise, knowledge, or creativity to elevate the ordinary. This isn't to slight any designers out there, but this is a book for directors, and you need to be well versed in all these disciplines in the event any of your designers aren't. If they're wonderful, great, then you are merely collaborating—which is what any good theater production is based on. But if they are more technical than creative, or merely novices, then it falls to you to pick up the slack.

As for me, if I didn't get involved in all the technical aspects I'd be denying myself one of the true joys of the creative process, and would not feel I have put my directorial stamp on the entire show.

Properties

Working hand in hand with the properties master or mistress is yet another area where a director's input is quite important. Some scripts provide a prop list based on the original show, other scripts provide no list whatsoever. Occasionally props will be mentioned in a stage direction, but that will be minimal at best. It is the director's and stage manager's jobs to provide an accurate, working prop list, and since it can change, evolve, and develop throughout the early rehearsals, additions, deletions, and other changes must be communicated ASAP to the prop people. As producer I sometimes have a cutoff date for new props, much to the chagrin of a director, simply because it isn't fair to the prop people to make demands at the last minute. I will bend that rule, of course, but it gives the director an idea of how important it is to have a prepared prop list that is as precise as possible in order to ensure that you'll get the right things. It is not acceptable simply to say that four chairs are needed and expect the prop people to read your mind. What type of chairs? Red kitchen chairs from the '50s? Bentwood chairs painted purple? Leather armchairs? Schoolhouse chairs? You need to be specific. In fact, finding a photo on the Internet is best of all. Props have to be borrowed, rented, bought, or even built and wasting time and money with insufficient information is not a good thing.

I make up a chart in Excel, which has the following columns: Act and Scene; Prop Needed; Amount Needed; Description of Prop (this is a wide column!); Actor Who Uses Prop (if applicable); Where It Is Preset (sometimes referred to as where it "lives"); and then, for the propsters' convenience, I might add two columns, Vendor (where they can put from where they are going to get the prop) and Secured, to indicate whether it has been obtained.

Props fall into two categories: hand props and set props. Hand props are those used or held by an actor—everything from a gun to an umbrella to a pair of glasses to a custard pie. Set props are those items that dress the stage or sets, and can include chairs, beds, floral arrangements, window dressings, and so on. A typewriter would be a set prop rather than hand prop, even though it is used by an actor.

The director most certainly would be responsible for providing the list and descriptions of the hand props. If the theater hires a set decorator, or the set designer wants to handle decoration, then the director would work in collaboration. Like costumes, props may be rented, bought, built, or borrowed. Sometimes you'll be afforded rehearsal props, which are facsimiles of the real ones. But more often you won't, and will have to make do with what's around the rehearsal space.

For me, a director/set designer/producer, one of the most rewarding portions of the creation process is dressing the stage and sets. This is where my attention to detail pays off, where I can help create an environment that brings the play to life. For example, I recently had the occasion of finishing the dressing-room sets for *Kiss Me, Kate* here at my theater. The two units were built on wagons (castered platforms); one had a four-by-eight-foot footprint, and the other was built on a four-by-twelve-foot wagon. They each had doors that led supposedly to the "outside" and a connecting door between them. The process of taking the bare walls and floor and turning them into a lived-in environment was great fun.

We used some old linoleum that looked remarkably like a wood floor to cover the top of the platforms (the floors of the dressing rooms)—we found the linoleum at a garage sale for about three dollars. Using joint compound from the hardware store, we "spackled" sections of the walls to make them look old and rundown—this method, coupled with creative scenic painting, works outstandingly well and is inexpensive. We scanned photos of old theatrical posters from various theater books, brought them into Photoshop, added the names of the actors in our show, and printed them out on eleven-by-seventeen-inch and seventeen-by-twenty-two-inch sheets of paper. If you don't have a printer that can do this, you can take the graphic files to a Kinko's or some other printing house. Thin pieces of molding were used to create frames for these "posters." Also on the computer, we created fake telegrams and printed them out on yellow paper. We have a collection of glass doorknobs and brass key plates, so we used those. We created old-style radiators out of wood and attached painted PVC pipe and elbows to them to give the feeling of the indoor heating and plumbing. Shelves were added to both dressing rooms and stocked with hatboxes, wigs on wig heads, ties and belts and boas. We glued ripped sections of kraft paper to parts of the walls and peeled it away. When the walls were painted to resemble wallpaper, it appeared as if the paper was ripped and peeling in sections. The finishing touches were the chair rail and wainscoting (all made from Styrofoam), practical wall sconces, a three-panel dressing screen and the makeup tables. Overflowing garbage cans and scattered garments completed the effect. It was an afternoon well spent and provided the actors with a realistic and atmospheric environment.

Sound

Of all the theatrical disciplines, to me, sound is the most elusive. With lighting, you point the instrument, see where the light falls, and work with it. The sets are about lumber and canvas and paint. And costumes are tangible. But sound is invisible, and the equipment that amplifies it is, at best, sensitive.

Your involvement with the sound designer might be as simple as suggesting and indicating sound effects, or as complicated as advising which actor should get a body microphone. Depending on the venue, you may or may not need microphones. Straight plays often can do without, or can suffice with a few floor microphones along the apron. Larger theaters doing musicals, with orchestras, might need to buy or rent wireless body microphones.

At my theater, we use wireless microphones, which are hard enough to control if you are inside but, being outside, as we are, they are next to impossible. On weekends, the local television stations boost their signals, which wreak havoc with us. If the air is heavy or has too much moisture, or if there is static electricity in the air, the microphones might act up. If an actor sweats, the microphone elements can be ruined. Proper placement of the microphone—whether in the hair or over the ear of the actor (lapels never work)—is always a challenge. And mixing all those microphones along with an orchestra and sound effects is the most daunting chore in theater.

Therefore, my advice to a director is, if microphones are called for, hire the best person you can afford for the job and leave it to them. Yes, you can be helpful by telling the sound designer when there are lines being shouted offstage, or when there are sudden entrances he needs to be aware of, and where the sound effects occur, but otherwise, let him or her do his or her thing.

You can, however, help the sound person with the job by clarifying things for the actors. One thing the actors need to start to rehearse right from the first is to know that they need to *not talk* for at least ten seconds after they make an exit. They need to give the designer and board operator a chance to turn their microphones off.

I have a classic story that exemplifies my point, but the language is raw. I'm going to tell it anyway, but I'll bleep the words. The show was *Me and My Girl* at a local college. The actress playing Lady Jacqueline had just finished a big number and she, as well as the ensemble, exited grandly into the wings, leaving the actor playing the Solicitor alone on stage. The minute she hit the wings, she said in the loudest possible voice, "S—t, I have to p—s like a f—ing racehorse!" Her microphone was still on and her voice rang through loud and clear. It was like attending a performance of *Springtime for Hitler*—we all sat there with our mouths open. The poor Solicitor didn't quite know what to do, so he pretended nothing happened—brave soul. I think the actress probably learned her lesson. Proving it's good to practice discipline right from the start.

If you are in a situation where you don't need body microphones, you may still require some sound effects or background music. While this is not something you have to be involved in creating—although if you are technically inclined you just might—it is still helpful for you to know some of what goes into creating audio tracks for theater. You might even find yourself working with a composer who is writing original music or scoring your show in some way, or you might be choosing very specific preshow, intermission, postshow, curtain call, and other underscoring music selections.

In the old days, reel-to-reel tape recorders were used, and these actually worked well. Cassettes worked less effectively because queuing them up was a nightmare. Carts were then introduced in the professional market, but with the advent of the digital revolution, where home enthusiasts can edit DV videotape and make DVDs, the two methods of choice today seem to be either minidisks or CDs. Minidisks had a brief run as a home audio product, but now, with the iPod and MP3 digital music, they are relegated to pro use primarily. What's nice about the minidisk is the ability to cue up a track so easily, plus the fact that you can rerecord on minidisk and visually label each track that shows up on the CDs work well too, but cueing is a tad more awkward. Both methods produce excellent stereo sound, and can be created with pro-amateur equipment and computers.

In conclusion, whether you are hired for a situation where you are in charge of virtually everything, or you are working in an ideal situation where your primary concern is the staging and acting, having knowledge of the tech side of things will go a long way to ensuring the success of the production and will allow you to communicate with the designers in their language. The more research you have done, and the more you have thought through everything technical, the better you can express these ideas to the designers. The more you communicate, and the more you understand their designs, the better you can block and stage the show. When the inevitable madness of tech week arrives, the more prepared you are and the better you understand going into tech what to expect, the more you can minimize the ordeal. If you can explain to the actors at each step what they can expect from sets, costumes, props, and even lighting and sound, the better the whole experience will be. Research and communication is always the key—and pay attention to the details. Let that be your mantra.

8

The Rehearsal Period

The First Rehearsal

Once the show has been cast and you've had all the preproduction meetings with your designers, you can look ahead to the first rehearsal. It has long been a tradition that the first rehearsal is a read-through, with the cast sitting around a big table or in a circle and just reading through the script. If it is a musical, the musical director might also play through the songs, and those who are familiar with the score would sing along.

I have no intention of robbing anyone of this time-honored practice, but unless there is an abundance of rehearsal time, this is a step I skip. I can understand doing a reading with a new show that no one has read or seen, but if the play is generally familiar and time is short, I would start with blocking if it is a straight play, or with music rehearsals if the show is a musical.

There is another reason for skipping the read-through in amateur productions. Despite the fact that you might announce that the read-through is purely for the sake of becoming familiar with the show—and is *not* an acting exercise—amateur actors often feel that they have to deliver a "performance" during the read-through, and that they are being judged by their peers, some of whom covet their roles. And sometimes this is unfortunately true. The read-through also occurs prior to your explanations and guidance on character and interpretation—yet another reason for you to skip the process.

If you are directing an Equity production, I can see where a read-through might not only be expected, but beneficial. The Equity actors might very well be more seasoned, and thus won't fall into some of the traps I've mentioned. They will use the read-through as a way to bond with each other and to get excited about the rehearsal process that lies ahead. It provides a means to get a feel for the emotional depth of the show, or to discover where the comedy lies, especially if the show is not one repeatedly performed. The read-through will also allow the director to sit back and observe, making mental notes on challenges that he or she might face.

But there is value in having the entire cast present at this first meeting. It presents an opportunity to pass out contact sheets that the SM has prepared, containing pertinent information and contact numbers for all the performers and key personnel. Most important on the contact sheet is a phone number where actors can call if they are caught in traffic or detained for some other reason. This might be the theater phone if there is line that will ring through to the rehearsal hall or, in this day and age of cell phones, perhaps the SM's cellular.

If you have a detailed rehearsal schedule already prepared, that would also be distributed. Creating a rehearsal schedule is a difficult, time-consuming, painstaking process in an amateur theater situation. With an Equity production you are more or less assured that every actor will be at every rehearsal—after all, they are getting paid to rehearse. But volunteer actors with day jobs, classes, prior commitments, and significant others will often present you with a daunting array of rehearsal conflicts. I have worked on shows where, after the first rehearsal, I did not have the entire cast again until the first night of tech. Tech week, for me, is sacrosanct. If an actor has conflicts with tech week, I generally will not cast them.

Your goal is to make up a schedule that doesn't waste the actors' time, capitalizes on who is available, and gets the production blocked as quickly and efficiently as possible so that run-throughs can begin. It is not an easy task. With a straight play it might mean working on small sections of the play at a time, perhaps going out of order. With a musical it could mean spending some rehearsals just on chorus numbers (ideally with a scene or two being blocked in another room), and other rehearsals just on scene work.

It's great for all involved if you indeed can stage the show in order, scene by scene, but that just isn't always possible. Strive for it—but be prepared for compromise. And be prepared for actors who suddenly forgot that they had a few additional conflicts. You might find yourself coming to rehearsal with one thing in mind, only to find that an actor or two won't be attending. Be ready to adjust. And take advantage of explaining to the cast just how important it is to be at rehearsal. It's not a case of preaching to the choir—it's showing by example how sudden absences can wreak havoc.

Regarding actors who miss rehearsals: I often hear them say things such as, "But I'm a quick learner and I'll pick up what I missed." It's hard to get through to such an actor that it isn't so much what he or she will miss as how it affects the rest of the cast. They are the ones put at a disadvantage by having to learn new blocking or choreography with a stand-in or the stage manager reading the lines. It isn't fair to them.

Then, of course, there is the issue of filling in the actor when they next attend rehearsal. Sure, a stage manager can give them the blocking or a dance captain can fill them in on the choreography, but nine times out of ten when they try to do the scene or dance with the rest of the cast, you'll wind up holding their hands through it anyway.

Last, without the actual actor at the blocking rehearsal, the director is put at a disadvantage because every actor's input can impact the initial staging of a scene. Someone standing in with a script is not the original actor interpreting the lines and the blocking. Any way you look at it, a missing actor costs the production time and energy. Stress that to your cast members.

The Rehearsal Schedule

Let's take a look at a fictitious rehearsal schedule for a musical that has six weeks to rehearse. I've put it in story form—for no particular reason except that I thought it might be fun. This particular theater rehearses its shows on the stage, and generally holds rehearsals Monday through Thursday evenings from 7:30 to 10:30 and Sunday afternoons from 1:00 until 7:00, which is when a nice large chunk can get accomplished.

The first Monday night was devoted to the initial get-together. A read-through was not scheduled, but the director assembled the entire cast and talked through his ideas of the show. They were going to do the show following the general concept of the original production. The stage manager handed out contact sheets and asked everyone to make sure their information was correct—if not, the actors were to hand back corrections and a new sheet would be distributed the following night as well as sent via email, since not everyone had to attend on Tuesday.

The stage manager also handed out the rehearsal schedule for the first week—through Sunday—and told everyone that next weeks' schedule would be emailed within a day or two as well. The schedule for the first week was as follows: Tuesday night the principals and supporting roles were called in to learn their music. Wednesday night the ensemble was called to learn their music. Thursday was for the entire cast—they would sing through the entire show from start to finish. Sunday afternoon the opening number would be choreographed from 1:00 to 3:00, and then incorporated into the first scene for the rest of the evening. Only those in act 1, scene 1 needed to attend.

The director explained that he (in this case, we'll make the director a "he" and the choreographer and musical directors "she's") would not attend the rehearsals on Tuesday and Wednesday night while the music was being learned, but that he and the stage manager would come Thursday to hear the final results. There really isn't any need for the director to sit through while the cast learns the music; these are perhaps the only two nights the director has off, so he might as well take advantage of them.

There were a few minor conflicts with some cast members, but nothing terrible—still, the director explained his position on unexcused absences to everyone. The stage manager then went through the theater's house rules regarding food and drink on stage (not allowed), smoking (allowed outside) and the telephones (local calls only).

The director had asked the set designer if he could bring the model of the set to the first rehearsal, and so he gathered everyone around and talked through how the set would be utilized. There is nothing quite as fascinating—and impressive—to a cast as a well-done, fully painted scale model of the set, and this was no exception. It energized everyone.

The director then went on to explain his working methods. He prefers to get the show blocked as quickly as possible because it wasn't until the run-through period that the real character work begins. He urged the cast to get "off book" (lines memorized) as soon as possible; in fact, a deadline was set for the third week of rehearsals. Basically, he explained, they would attempt to block the show over a three-week period, as well as work through all the musical numbers. A stumble-through[1] of the first act would be held as soon as act one was blocked. A stumble-through of act 2 would be held once it was on its feet. After that, it would be run-throughs each rehearsal, with one or two nights each week devoted to fixing problems and cleaning the choreography. The last week would be tech week. Additionally, there would be times when the costumer would be taking measurements and doing fittings when performers were not on stage, and scheduling would be worked around the rehearsals.

The director then mentioned that the Hollywood movie of the play was quite different from the script that they were working with. While it would be beneficial to watch it for a sense of the time period, a feeling of the costumes, and to note some good performances by the leading actors, it should not directly influence their show.

Last, since this was a cast of both experienced performers and novices, the director reviewed the vernacular he would be using during blocking, apologizing to those who were familiar with the terminology but explaining it would save time later if everyone was on the same page:

Stage left and stage right are from the actor's point of view—the onus is on the director to reverse things from the audience.

Upstage is toward the back wall; *downstage* is toward the apron of the stage.

There were three sets of *legs* (thin, velour curtains that mask the wings or offstage areas) and they defined the offstage areas moving from downstage to upstage. Thus, an actor making an entrance or exit from between the proscenium and the first set of legs was entering or exiting *in one; in two* was between the second and third legs and *in three* was upstage of the third set of legs.

The area downstage of the proscenium (the plaster arch that defines the edge of the stage) is the *apron*.

---

1 A stumble-through is a rehearsal in which the entire act is run from beginning to end without stopping so that everyone involved can get a sense of continuity and the creative staff can see where the problems are.

That seemed to be enough information to start with—other explanations and terminology would come up during rehearsals.

The director wanted to explain one other thing before the rehearsal was over, and that was the method by which he preferred to give, and for the actors to take, notes. Notes would be given at the end of a rehearsal or run-through, and he expected all the actors to come to the note session with paper and pencil. Notes were to be jotted down and not left to memory. The director also explained that he preferred the actor to take the notes without comment (pros usually say, "thank you" as well after being given a note) because a performer defending or justifying his mistake or blaming the problem on someone or something else wastes too much time. Furthermore, an actor who debates notes is usually too busy talking to actually hear and absorb them. Asking for clarification is one thing—and appropriate—but defensiveness is unnecessary.

The director further explained that notes, by their very nature, usually point to those things that need work and that there simply wasn't time to add much positive reenforcement in the note sessions. That would be reserved for emails the next day. And everyone was expected to listen to *all* the notes; very often there is information to be learned by all even when just one person is being addressed. This speech would bear repeating after the first run-through, at note-giving time.

Since there was only about an hour left of the rehearsal period, the director dismissed everyone but the two main leads, who stayed for the rest of the period to work with the musical director.

The director and choreographer finalized the rest of the rehearsal schedule over the next two days so that it was ready to give out on Thursday night. The second week of rehearsals was heavy with choreography since it was felt that the sooner the dance routines were learned the better—some of the harder numbers could be run first thing each night before the blocking began.

At the first Sunday's rehearsal, the director got to work with the cast for the first time. The director's way of working was to explain the blocking a few lines at a time, then let the actors get up and try it. Then he'd explain a few more lines. Sometimes, if something were a bit tricky, he'd demonstrate it. Then, after a few pages were completed, he would run what had been blocked thus far. This continued until the scene was finished.

The stage manager notated every blocking move as well as what props were required, in pencil (since it was apt to change) in the prompt script. The prompt script tended to look like a football play, with circles representing actors and lines and arrows showing their moves. Occasionally, an actor suggested an alternative piece of blocking or asked if they might try interpreting something slightly different, and because the director believed that everything was worth at least a look, it was allowed. The director would then decide if the suggestion was indeed an improvement or if the original idea was the one that worked best. This is one of those times that test a director's people skills. The director wants to create an atmosphere of collaboration where the performer is free to experiment and contribute, but must also maintain control. Some actors will make a suggestion and not think twice if the director dismisses it; others will test the water to see how far they can go. Some actors will question everything while others are willing to try whatever is suggested.

After a few rehearsals, the director got to know the personalities of the cast and adapted his methods to each of them—firm but gentle with some, cajoling with others, and genuinely interested with many. As rehearsals progressed, the director also got a feeling for the rate at which the actors progressed, noting that some grasped the blocking, characterization, and stage business right off while others needed constant reminders, review, and explanations.

One of the problems, he learned, was that there were a few actors who could not readily adapt to change, so the blocking and business he gave them right from the start had to be worked out in advance. Even so, there were times when, despite some actors' inability to adapt easily to change, change was simply dictated. When this occurred the director would explain the changes slowly, then have the stage manager review the new blocking or business in another room so that the main stage could be used for other things. Positive reenforcement was called for when working with actors who had difficulty changing what they initially learned.

This particular director came to rehearsal well prepared, and had two approaches. For some intricate scenes, he would block the movement at home and come to the rehearsal with every movement choreographed, ready to teach the cast. For other scenes, he would merely have a basic idea of the scene's progression and allow the actors to organically feel the dynamics of the scene. After a few improvisations, the director would "cement" what he liked the best, and that would go into the prompt book.

There are pros and cons to both methods of directing—coming prepared with every "beat" worked out in advance or merely having a general idea of the scene's needs and allowing it to develop during the rehearsal. Both methods work, but not for every play and not for every group of actors or every director.

The director who works everything out in advance, down to hand movements, instills in his cast a feeling that he has a distinct vision and is completely in control. For an actor, knowing that the director is prepared—and thus time won't be wasted—is a very positive aspect. This approach is often mandated for an Equity rehearsal period where time is money and you are working with professionals. For a director who does not feel comfortable improvising and thinking on his feet, the more preparation done as homework, the more confident he will be. Often, this type of director will watch what he has created—perhaps even videotape it— and then go home to review it, coming back the next day with changes. The main drawback here is that if the actors are used to improvising or making suggestions, they might feel less creative. This might tend to throw the director and give the actors the impression that the director is not open to any input from the cast.

The other extreme is illustrated by a director who does not plan out any of the blocking or business beforehand, but, rather, works on his feet. If the director is adept at this method, it can be exciting and creative. However, this can only work when there is an abundance of time and a cast that is comfortable with this style. It is important that the director not appear unprepared, unsure, or confused, for this will not instill confidence in the actors, who will feel their time is being wasted. This could also give them too much power, which can lead to their trying to direct the show themselves.

For me, a combination of both methods, dictated by the type of show and the cast, works best. In a musical or a slapstick comedy where stylization and crisp, clean blocking is called for, the director should come to rehearsal having completely worked out everything in advance. In a drama with a small cast where reality is called for, an organic, improvisational approach might work out perfectly well.

Back to staging our musical. The director and choreographer decided ahead of time that the director would stage or "choreo-

graph" the ballads in the show, freeing the choreographer to con-
centrate on the large, "dancier" numbers. There were two solo ballads in the first act, so the director put those numbers "on their
feet." Although the director was certainly neither a dancer nor a
choreographer, he had enough experience staging musicals that he
felt comfortable with this procedure. But he made it clear to the
actors that once they had learned what he had given them, the
choreographer would watch the song, "clean it," and perhaps
embellish it with additional movement. This is so that the whole
production looked seamless and the ballads do not stick out from
the rest of the musical numbers. At the end of the second week, act
1 was completely blocked, but since it had been staged out of order,
there was no sense of continuity. The first stumble-through was
scheduled for Sunday at one.

A stumble-through is both exciting and nerve-wracking.
Undoubtedly it will be choppy and there will be lots of things
forgotten, but it can give the cast an idea of the big picture, and
while it might take three hours to get through a one-hour act, with
any luck there is a real sense of accomplishment at the end of
rehearsal. This one lived up to tradition—there were plenty of rough
moments, many bits were forgotten, and some of the choreography
fell apart, but in general, everyone felt that act 1 basically worked.

With the third week approaching, act 2 could be finished and
still leave time for a music brush-up and a chance to review some
of act 1's choreography and forgotten moments. But then the unex-
pected happened. On Tuesday of the third week one of the supporting actors was forced to quit the production. She had an ailing
relative out of state and would have to leave.

Going back to the audition forms proved valuable, because
there were two alternate choices that might be right for the show.
But there was also an actress in the ensemble who had come close
to getting this particular role, and certainly could perform it. This
forced a meeting because a choice had to be made. One the one
hand, if someone outside the cast was brought in, none of the production numbers would have to be changed due to the "upgrad-
ing" of one of the dancers, which would certainly save time. The
supporting role that needed to be filled was only in one of the big
numbers. But, on the other hand, the ensemble member was very
familiar with the blocking and business for the supporting role, and
really wanted a chance to prove herself.

After careful consideration, and weighing time against morale, it was decided to move the ensemble member up into the supporting role, and replace the dancer instead. At the heart of this decision was the boost it gave the cast, who wanted to feel that the creative staff cared enough to consider the feelings of the ensemble member even if it meant more work for the choreographer. Show biz is full of stories of the chorus member who makes it big, and in their own little world, this was happening. To ease the workload, two of the other ensemble members agreed to serve as dance captains and teach the new "kid" all the choreography outside of the normal rehearsal schedule.

The third week of rehearsals chugged along fine, and at the end there was a stumble-though of act 2, which went quite well. By this time the creative staff and the performers had gotten to know what to expect from each other and had reached comfortable working conditions. The fourth and fifth weeks were spent alternating between full run-throughs and brush-up, cleaning rehearsals. One of the early run-throughs was dedicated to acting moments. Skipping the musical numbers, the director took the cast slowly through each scene, stopping when any actor had a question about motivation, character development, line readings, or interpretation. This proved extremely valuable and straightened out a number of rough edges. Striving for clarity was the goal of this rehearsal and it worked.

Another rehearsal was dedicated pretty much to set shifts. Even though there weren't yet any sets to shift, the director assigned the set moves to particular actors at the conclusion of each scene or number and walked through the way in which the sets would be brought on and off, discussing how to do it in character. The choreographer added some flair to the shifts as well. This preparation would go a long way to helping make tech week run smoother.

Yet another rehearsal was devoted to props. The action was halted at each juncture when a major prop was used, to make sure the actor knew exactly what the prop was, how it was to be used and, of equal importance, where and how the prop was to be stored. Was it something already on the set; was it to be brought on by the actor from an offstage prop table; or was it to be handed to the actor by a stagehand in the wings? The stage manager made notes as to all the decisions regarding props.

There was even a rehearsal during which the focus was the accuracy of the lines. The actors sat around the stage and delivered their lines from a seated position while the SM followed along on book. The idea was to pick up the *cues*—not to say the lines in a hurried manner but to reduce the time between when one actor stopped speaking and the next began. This, as well as checking for accuracy, proved very valuable at the next run-through. Keeping the pace up during a scene is often a case of reducing the gaps between lines rather than speeding up a delivery. A fine point, to be sure, but an important one. Speeding up the deliveries results in confusion and misunderstood thoughts—but closing the gaps keeps the pace bright.

As the last week of rehearsals approached the director felt the show was in the right shape to face the decisive chapter—the tech. He had held a final mandatory and complete production meeting so that everyone knew exactly what to expect during tech. The actors were off book (their lines memorized), the choreography and musical numbers were clean and polished, and everyone was ready to deal with props and sets. Tech week is always a challenge, but the obstacles had been minimized by communication and preparation.

Summary

I'll save the adventures of tech week for another chapter and will close my little novella here. Hopefully it has provided a rough blueprint for scheduling and running your rehearsal period. Of course, there are as many variations on this theme as there are plays and directors, but the basic scheduling should hold true. If you are directing a straight play, there are a number of steps you can obviously eliminate, and the rehearsal weeks can be fewer, but the same procedures for dealing with both actors and creative staff remain unchanged.

One difference, however, in rehearsing a nonmusical lies in some of the directorial techniques used with the actors. Unlike musicals, straight plays frequently have a less-rigid rehearsal schedule and, thus, the luxury of discovering the characters in a more leisurely manner. This might manifest itself in acting exercises, both physical and intellectual.

One such mental exercise involves past lives. The actors go home and write up a biography of sorts in which they create and describe aspects of their character's life prior to when we find them in the play. They write, perhaps in a journal, all about their parents and siblings, schooling and hobbies, events that happened as they were growing up, and influences that impacted their current state in the comedy or drama. Depending on the experience and discipline of the actor, this can be very helpful in developing a multidimensional character. If you know how you got where you are, you can better predict your character's reactions to the situations presented by the playwright.

Another improvisational exercise takes place "at a party" in a home where actors come in character. They then improvise how their characters might interact in an unscripted situation. This helps them think like the character and become more natural on stage. I find that this exercise can't go on for too long or it falls apart, but a half hour or so can serve the purpose, then everyone can relax and just socialize.

Whether these and other acting exercises work for you is very subjective. It takes a special group of actors to benefit from them; others may find them foolish, embarrassing, or unproductive. Certainly they work in an academic environment (college and even high school) but might not be greeted with enthusiasm in every community theater.

Even without acting exercises, a straight play provides you with the time to fully explore characterizations to an extent not often possible when trying to create a musical. Experimentation and discovery is the key—allowing the actors to try many different interpretations of a scene, a line delivery, or their characters in general. The director will then finally settle and "cement" the interpretation that works best. Encouraging the actors to explore and try different things is one of the great joys of directing, and a skillful director will know when the right choice has finally been made.

My choreographer, Michelle, and I always breathe a sigh of relief when the blocking rehearsals are over and the dances have been taught because that's when the real collaborative creativity begins between the directors and the actors. The few weeks (or days) between teaching the blocking and beginning tech is the time for the director and cast to really explore the show—pulling apart each scene and discussing every delivery, every bit of blocking, every nuance. Come tech week, there are so many other concerns that the wise and experienced director will seize this interim period and take full advantage of the time. Whether you have a run-through planned or just want to work individual scenes, this is the time to experiment, play, develop, take chances, rework, and deconstruct. Use it while you can—the dreaded tech week approaches!

9

Tech Week

The time spent finally adding together all things technical has come to be known as tech week—or, as they say on the West End of London, "technicals." Whether tech week actually lasts seven days or not isn't relevant. What is relevant is that it begins the most difficult of times. These are the rehearsals where the following elements are introduced:

- Costumes, along with the associated costume changes, quick changes, accessories, wigs, and makeup.
- Lighting, encompassing general lighting, specials, follow spots, intelligent moving lights, fog machines, and hazers or other special effects; plus marking areas of the stage with spike tape so that actors hit their mark when specialty lighting is involved.
- Sets, including soft goods (curtains, drops, travelers, headers, and legs), and hard goods (a turntable, wagons, muslin-covered flats, doors, windows—you name it). This heading also includes moving (or shifting, as it is called) the sets about from one scene to the next.
- Sound, both sound reinforcement with microphones and sound effects and music.
- Orchestra, if it is a musical. This can be merely the addition of drums and bass or a full complement of musicians—regardless, it is going to sound different from the solo rehearsal pianist.

The first night of tech is liable to be the most confusing. This is particularly evident if the show has been rehearsing in a rehearsal hall.

At Plays-in-the-Park, only the first show of the summer has the luxury of rehearsing on the stage. As each show runs ten nights with a one-and-a-half-week tech turn-around between shows, the other shows rehearse at a local college and don't set foot on the actual stage until the first tech rehearsal. The first night is spent adapting the show to the space; in fact, often we only get through act 1 on the first night and save act 2 until the next evening. If a show has been rehearsing elsewhere, there are all sorts of considerations to deal with besides the technical elements. Entrances and exits will be slightly different, the upstage/downstage dimensions will have changed and will need adaptation, and all the spatial relationships will be confusing. If you have been rehearsing elsewhere, you might need to consider an additional tech night just to solve these issues.

Here is an example of what a tech schedule might look like, assuming you are working on a musical. I give two different examples of how the first night might be run, depending on whether you have been at the theater all along or are just moving in after rehearsing elsewhere.

Evening One (Rehearsing at the Theater All Along)

Since you have been at the theater all along, you can jump right into tech. The first step is to introduce to your actors a whole new slew of people whom they will now be working with hand in hand: the volunteer backstage crew. While every show and theater vary to some degree, you might make use of some, if not all, of the following positions:

Crew Chief Works hand in hand with the director and stage manager in managing the set shifts. Usually, he or she lives backstage and is the direct report to the shift crew. The crew chief wears a wireless headset, if available, tied to an intercom system (most often made by Clear-Com) so that he can hear cues called by the stage manager. If only a wired headset is available, then some sort of tally light will have to be rigged to tell the crew chief to pick up the headset.

Shift Crew Any number of people whose purpose it is to move the sets around. If actors are utilized to move the set pieces on stage, then the shift crew gets everything ready behind the scenes, in the wings. If actors aren't used, then the shift crew—either in black or costumed—do the actual moving.

Prop Runners   These folks handle the props—presetting them before the show, resetting them after the show is over, and handing them to actors or collecting them in the wings (handoffs).

Dressers   Costume-oriented workers who help the actors with quick changes and other costume and makeup needs.

Wardrobe Master or Mistress   Person in charge of the dressers; also directly handles the laundry or supervises it.

Microphone Technicians   People who help get body microphones on the performers properly.

Board Operator   Someone who operates the lighting board at the stage manager's commands.

Follow-Spot Operators   An obvious assignment; depending on the theater, could be one person or as many as four or more.

Remember: many of these people are volunteers, unless the theater is very well endowed, and as such, they need to be respected. There needs to be a symbiotic relationship between the actors and them—especially the prop people, dressers, and microphone staff. I explain that yes, the actors are volunteers as well, but they reap the benefits of the applause, while the backstage crew has a somewhat thankless job—unless, of course, we thank them.

I also explain to the actors that until the entire tech is completed and everything is set in stone and operating smoothly, the production staff—especially the electricians and shift crew—should be given the right of way backstage. They are moving heavy pieces of scenery and delicate and expensive pieces of equipment, and trying to move these items without ripping drops or other soft goods. So the actors should allow them to pass, even if it means initially being late for an entrance or having an exit blocked. It'll all eventually work out.

Introductions made, it's time to begin. The play has to start somehow, so setting up exactly how it will begin is an obvious place to start. Will there be a curtain speech by the producer or a board member? If so, that will cue everything else. If not, then the houselights dimming to half could signal the start of the show.

Then they would go out completely, leaving the exposed stage or the main curtain lit in the preset, which then also slowly goes out, and the show begins. House to half. House out. Preset out. Lights up on act 1, scene 1, or the overture, whichever applies.

Sounds good, doesn't it? But I'm a little ahead of myself. The lighting designer isn't ready to lay in some cues yet, so this is something you will verbalize to the cast, so they know how the show will kick off. In actuality, the first tech rehearsal will go from scene to scene, while you talk through difficult set changes and then try them out, making sure you have enough people to execute them. The lighting designer will be watching intently, confirming that he or she has the right lights set up to do the job.

There are several approaches to getting the lights done, and the director and lighting designer will want to work out the best approach for the theater and the show. One way would be to hold a dry tech during which the lighting designer and director, along with some technicians, go through the show and set all the lighting looks and cues without actors—perhaps during an afternoon early on in the tech process. Then, on the second night of tech, the light design is "tried out" on the show and tweaked, starting and stopping the action when necessary.

Another approach would be to devote the second night of rehearsal to a *cue to cue.* A cue-to-cue rehearsal, which does involve the actors, is a rehearsal where you don't concern yourself with scenery, props, or costumes but jump to every point in the show where a lighting cue happens, set the cue, then jump to the next one. The actors only say those lines or do those sections of songs that involve a lighting change of some sort.

The third approach is to have the designer create the lighting design "on the fly," progressing along night after night while everything else happens. This is the option many times in outdoor theaters where you cannot do any lighting during the day. After a few nights, the LD might ask to halt the action when he needs to tweak something.

Regardless of the approach, the director will want to keep a keen eye on what is happening, because it is easier to correct a missed cue or incorrect look as it happens (or in notes after the rehearsal) than to notice it many rehearsals later.

Regarding notes, here's an approach that works for me. During the course of tech rehearsals, you or your assistant will be taking a myriad of notes—tech notes for the staff and acting notes for the performers. I use a laptop computer, and find it helpful to set up a Word document with a table that has two cells, left and right. On the left side I list each department: props, electrics, sets, costumes, producer, crew chief, and so forth. In the right-hand column I type in all my notes to the various departments. I print it out at the end of rehearsal and distribute it in cubby-holes (which could be file folders, mail boxes, Lucite bins, or a variation) I have set up in a common area at the theater and designated for the designers and crew chiefs to pick up before the next day's work.

I use my laptop for the actors, too, but for a different reason. Normally I gather everyone together after rehearsal and read the notes, but on those occasions when we run very late or I feel reenforcement is necessary, I can email the notes easily to everyone that night or the next day, since they are already in an electronic form.

Evening One (First Night at the Actual Theater)

Assemble the cast and talk them through what to expect over the coming week. The theater will most likely have some rules and regulations concerning food, smoking, parking, dressing rooms, and backstage guests, among other things, and this would be a good time to review them.

Tech can be fraught with down time for the actors, so it is important to explain that (a) they should bring a good book or homework to rehearsals for the times when they have to wait (or even study their scripts!) and (b) they must be within earshot because they might be called on to either do a scene or shift a set at a moment's notice.

Once everyone understands what to expect, it's time to plow in. On this first night, it might be advantageous to go through the entire show from the beginning with the sole purpose of making sure all the blocking and choreography fits the space properly. You might find spots in the show where you thought you had more room, and spots where you thought you had less. This could require some restaging. Choreography might have to be adapted to fill a larger space, or compressed if space is restricted. This requires that the actors adjust and, in some cases, relearn what they had been rehearsing for many weeks, so go slow, be patient, and ask for their patience. The fact that they are excited about the new theater space can mask and diminish some of the changes, especially if you present it in the light of how much better it will be. With any luck, there won't be anything beyond control that you'll be up against.

Keep in mind that the lighting designer, prop people, crew chief, and other shift crew should all watch this rehearsal—taking advantage of the one night they will get to see the show without actually "working" it. They surely would have sat in on a few prior rehearsals, but possibly not as a collective entity. Once the show has been adapted, the rest of the rehearsal week can go as outlined.

Days Two, Three, and Four

Each evening I try to add a new technical element to the rehearsal, staggered, so that the evening's purpose is clear and focused. Since the set might not be completed by the time the first tech rehearsal rolls around, we find more and more of it completed each night and must add that into the rehearsal. The second night, we add all props—stopping anytime necessary to decide where the prop will "live" (onstage, or offstage on a prop table) or when a prop is missing or not quite right. The third night is usually devoted to costumes. Adding the costumes can take a long time, since no one can judge how long it will take to make costume changes until they actually do it. Leave extra time—and find extra patience—for this night. The fourth night might be the night that you will actually stop and start for lighting cues and effects, if you haven't already. In many circumstances you will also have the orchestra or rhythm section (piano, bass, drums, and guitar) playing for the first time.

By now, with any luck, you have worked out the following:

- Starting the show, ending act 1, starting act 2, ending the show, and curtain calls
- Storage of the set pieces in the wings and a logistical manner to facilitate their shifts on- and offstage
- Details of shifting the set pieces on and off the stage for each scene
- Opening and closing of any curtains and traveler drops
- Storing, placing, and using all props

- All costume changes, including accessories, wigs, and makeup
- Use of the body microphones, if applicable, and all sound effects
- Any special effects and/or video or slide-show use.

If all has gone as planned, you have also had an opportunity to watch the show once or twice with all these pieces in place, providing an opportunity for you to revisit all your directorial choices and make sure your original ideas have been implemented and are working as anticipated.

The night before the final dress I will also approach the cast. I tell them that tonight or tomorrow during the day they should all pick up the script again and read it from cover to cover as if for the first time. Chances are they will each suddenly find that there is a word they are saying wrong, or a phrase they have inverted. It's a good exercise and very helpful in fixing minor problems. Because they are used to saying things a certain way, when they read something different it'll stand out.

The Final Dress

This is your final shot at fixing things. I certainly don't mean to imply that you cannot continue to give notes and to tweak throughout the run of the show, but in many cases the show lasts only three performances or the director is off and running after opening night. I know that some directors try to avoid stopping the show during a dress to fix something, but better to interrupt the rehearsal than to have a performance suffer.

This is also the time to watch the show for one of the most important aspects of all—the pacing. Ideally, this has been something that you have been aware of from the very first stumble-through, but tech rehearsals can often throw a monkey wrench in the pacing. Here is an opportunity to see, with everything running as smoothly as possible, where lines need to be picked up or scene changes tightened.

Of course, it is too late to make drastic cuts in the material if something isn't working; with luck, any serious trimming of dance music and the like was done during the first week. The final dress is the time to tighten those seemingly insignificant moments that have been bothering you. The point is, one tiny moment may seem insignificant, *but* twenty such tiny moments add up to a serious pacing problem over the course of the evening.

The type of moment I am referring to might occur during a line delivered by an actor taking too long a pause midsentence. It might be a moment where an actor is uncomfortable with a bit of business involving a prop and thus fumbles with it. Maybe it is a scene between two or more people where the dialogue should be rapid-fire but instead contains gaps in the rhythm. Again, individually they may not seem so bad; cumulatively they hurt the show's overall pace.

The question sometimes arises as to whether the dress rehearsal should include an audience—perhaps invited friends of the performers or members of the board. I have very mixed feelings about this. On the one hand, having an audience can tip you off to a number of things. Their reaction can tell you and the actors where the laughs are, whether the audience seems involved with the story, whether they applaud at the intended moments, and whether you keep their attention. If the audience comprises people whose opinions you value, then talking with them afterward can provide some insight into what works and what doesn't.

On the other hand, dress rehearsals are often fraught with mistakes and less-than-optimal performances, pacing, scene shifts, and costume changes. Despite the fact that you might tell the audience in your curtain speech that this is a dress rehearsal and what they are about to witness might indeed be rough, sometimes the damage is done, and you'll find out later that this preview audience has told their friends that the show needed work, or wasn't quite ready, or something on that order. This negative word-of-mouth can hurt ticket sales, and might never have happened if the people had attended a scheduled performance. I don't have the answer here, and caution you to weigh the pros and cons. Your own experience will dictate the way to go.

Conclusion

Tech week can be hell week. The hours are often very, very long. By the time you run the show and give notes, the witching hour may have come and gone. That's why Equity provides for one or more

10-out-of-12-hour rehearsals. When you are down to the wire, you simply have to stay until it gets done, solved, finished. But a good director can minimize the trauma of tech by being prepared and by making sure all the other departments are prepared as well. Here are some things to think about:

- Make sure the crew knows that a 7 P.M. go means a 7 P.M. GO—this is not the time to start getting ready. If it takes an hour and a half to set up the tech table, hook up the Clear-Coms, and do a light check, then they have to start at 5:30 P.M.

- Assemble the cast after the rehearsal and repeat your "how to take good notes" speech so that valuable time isn't spent discussing things that don't move the note session forward. Ask the actors to come to the session with a pad and pencil and to write down their notes. Ask them to not defend, argue, or talk through their notes. If they're busy doing any of the above, they are neither listening nor absorbing your note. And everyone should listen to all notes; sometimes a note given to an individual has value to the entire cast.

- Work out potential set shifts and prop moves beforehand with the actors and stage manager. Yes, you will have to adapt once you have the real items, but you won't be starting from scratch.

- Remind the cast of the hurry-up-and-wait syndrome, where they will find long stretches of time with nothing to do, only to suddenly be called onto the stage to quickly go to work.

- Keep things moving. Don't get bogged down in details that can be fixed at another time. Keep your eye on the time, and find a comfortable compromise between ignoring something that needs fixing and spending an inordinate amount of time fixing something that is less than crucial.

- As always, communicate. Even though you feel pressured and rushed, take the time to make sure everyone understands what you are saying. Whether it is a note to an actor or to a crew member, you'll save time if you are clearly understood the first time.

- Be flexible—have a plan in mind but be ready to adapt if necessary. If lights aren't ready but costumes are, go with it!

- Above all, take control! Too often tech rehearsals flounder because no one is sure who should take command. The director, with help from the stage manager, should keep everything moving along at a brisk but effective clip. Technicians can get bogged down in all things technical; actors tend to want to make sure their particular needs are met; musicians want to work on their stuff. The director needs to be the ringmaster who allows for all these concerns but makes sure they are time-frame appropriate while keeping the big picture in focus at all times.

- Always keep in mind that as you add each major element to the show, you can expect the actors to take a few backward steps until they are comfortable. Don't let it discourage you.

It occurs to me that the first act of *Noises Off* perfectly exemplifies the zaniness that is tech week. If you get a chance to see the show or even the movie, by all means do. And if you can ever direct it, jump on it. Bad dress rehearsal, good opening night. That's how the old adage goes, and I'd be lying if I didn't take some of these theatrical superstitions to heart. But that doesn't mean you hope for a bad dress, because a bad dress can also mean you're not ready, and that won't help the opening in the least.

10

Directing the Actors

I've kept this chapter toward the end of the book because it discusses perhaps the most challenging aspect of being a director, and the one about which I guess I'm most opinionated. It is possible for a director who knows nothing about anything technical to still pull off a good production if he knows how to handle the actors—after all, the tech could be left to the designers and technicians, but the acting can only be left to the director and the actors. This is where all your skills will come in to play: you'll double as a teacher, psychiatrist, traffic cop, disciplinarian, inspirational speaker, and best buddy. I felt it prudent to once again divide the chapter into venues, so you can jump right to the section that directly relates to your current job.

High School Theater

Directing on the high school level can provide one of the most satisfying and rewarding experiences, but it comes with a lot of responsibility. You are dealing with impressionable kids, and how you run the rehearsals and handle the performers can make the difference between instilling in a student a lifelong love for theater and turning them off to the theatrical arts forever.

There are two approaches to creating a high school show. One method is to cast as many students as possible, no matter their talent, in order to provide a theatrical experience for many. In this approach the outcome is not nearly as important as the involvement of as many students as feasible, as well as parents, teachers, and the community. It is an event, and if it is indeed a pleasant event, it will inspire many of the performers to pursue theater in college and in surrounding community theaters.

Many years ago, I sat across the desk from the superintendent of schools as he interviewed me for a high school directing job. He related a story to me from his days as a high school actor, when he was playing Zoltan Karpathy in *My Fair Lady*, a character who, traditionally, is bearded. He delighted in telling me how he ad-libbed on closing night, turning to the audience and exclaiming how his Shick razor gave him the closest shave—apparently paraphrasing a television commercial of the time. I didn't find that particularly amusing, but it demonstrated how this particular educator valued the experience over the integrity of the production. Nothing wrong with that. It is a choice, and one that can prove pleasing. If the right show is chosen—perhaps a musical with a large chorus—then by all means share the wealth if this is what you, and the school board, opt for.

The other method is to preserve the integrity of the show—to cast based on talent and what the role calls for—and keep the cast size appropriate. Direct the play as if it were a first-class Equity show, encouraging the kids to rise above ordinary high school productions and creating an environment of serious work. This will involve fewer students, but the trade-off is that those who are cast will walk away with a much more professional and realistic impression of what the real theater world is like.

Regardless of which style is chosen, the director must still be, above all, a teacher. Even students coming from experience in middle school or community theater will need to be taught the fundamentals of theater now that they are of an age where they can fully understand and appreciate them.

Whether you have cast a majority of seniors who have worked with you before, or a mixture of all grades, your first obligation is to teach the language of theater. You want the students to be familiar with the terms that they will hear repeatedly if they pursue the craft: *upstage* and *downstage, stage left* and *right, wings, borders, headers, teasers, drops, travelers, scrims, aprons*—all the terms that we take for granted but that might be new to so many of them. A chemistry teacher cannot assume every student knows what an Erlenmeyer flask is; a director cannot assume they know what a fiber-optic drop is.

Once everyone knows the language, blocking can begin. If ever there was an example of a director needing to have a grasp of the blocking right from the beginning it is in a high school show. Kids tend to latch on to what they are originally told, and even though you can most certainly make changes, if your first steps are solid the job will be easier. Go slow, explain everything clearly, and don't assume anything.

While you might be somewhat reluctant to try this with a seasoned professional, there is nothing wrong with demonstrating your thoughts for a high school actor. It often helps to jump up onto the stage and show the actor exactly what it is you're are looking for—high school kids get a kick out of having the director—their role model—up on stage with them, walking them, literally, through a scene.

I'm in my fifties, with a wealth of pop culture to pull from, and quite often find myself faced with blank stares when I refer to a movie, book, phrase, commercial, television show, or song that is more than fifteen years old. The first time I mentioned a record player, a few kids had no idea what I was talking about. But I feel that rather than give up on these references, it is better to make them and then send the cast scurrying off to Blockbuster to rent an old movie or dig up a book in a library. I'll even bring in videos from my personal collection and gather everyone around a VCR. The more you expand their points of reference, the more you connect them to the past, the more educated they will be in this particular craft.

Repetition is particularly helpful. Block out a small chunk of the action, then repeat and repeat it. With each successive repetition you'll see them advance, and you'll be able to add and embellish without overwhelming. A section of a scene that starts out with rudimentary blocking and stage business, will become, by the fifth pass, full and alive. Only then might you want to go on to the next section. It is also valuable to start each day with a quick review of what you did the day before. If you keep going forward without any review of what went before, the first stumble-through will be like reinventing the wheel. Chances are, many of them will have forgotten most of it.

Whatever you do, do it gently. Be kind and supportive. Your kids are going to be sensitive. They have chosen an extracurricular activity that sets them apart somewhat from the others in the school—unless, of course, you are directing at the High School of Performing Arts—so be receptive to that fact.

What happens when you get the occasional student who is disruptive and a troublemaker? Well, it might take a private meeting where you read him the riot act, or it might even take you having to set an example by having him leave the rehearsal. If the student is disruptive in all his school activities, it might be a disciplinary concern above and beyond the school play. Regardless, you must again exercise compassion.

Unique to a high school setting, you might find yourself in a close encounter with a parent, one who might be angry that their child was not cast, or didn't get the lead, or misconstrued something you said at rehearsal. You'll need to be calm and cool in such a situation, explaining your point of view and your reasoning in a polite but ultimately firm manner. If you do not establish your policies up front, the situation can escalate.

As with any cast, there will be those actors who take theater very seriously and those who are there for the fun and games. While this is certainly true in high school, you'll find that the majority take it seriously. You have an obligation to those serious students to nurture their love of theater and to support them. This is not to say that everyone is a future Al Pacino, but high school provides a good opportunity for them to explore whether they have what it takes—the talent, the stamina, and the perseverance.

I mentioned in my description of the various types of theaters that in the high school where I direct, I twice experimented with directing a small musical for the fall show instead of a drama. As this is a chapter about the actors, let me embellish by saying that doing these small musicals unfortunately excluded some potential theater students. While the small musicals were great fun for me and for the handful of talented triple-threat performers who could not only act but sing and dance as well, it precluded those kids who had not the talent for dance and singing but were very good actors. They would look forward each year to the drama or comedy because it gave them a chance to perform. So from some of the less musically inclined actors' points of view, these small musicals were a mixed blessing.

One last thought about directing on the high school level— you can sometimes have fun by going in an unusual direction with nontraditional casting to suit your potential acting candidates.

There will be years when you have strong girls to work with; years when the boys are better than the girls, and years when you have dancers, and years when you don't. Sometimes you need to pick a show that suits your talent pool. Neil Simon understood this, and took his most famous play, *The Odd Couple* and wrote a female version. And you can do that type of thing with other shows as well. I once directed *The Roar of the Greasepaint, The Smell of the Crowd* with a gender-bending cast and changed *Twelve Angry Men* to *Twelve Angry Jurors* to allow for a few females on the jury. These types of liberties are acceptable (if not totally legal) on a high school level.

In summary, keep in mind that you are forming the future for a great many theater kids, and since many are very vulnerable at this stage in their lives, you want to be sensitive, nurturing, encouraging, understanding, and above all, remember that you are as much a teacher as a director.

College Theater

What a difference a few years make. College theater is uniquely different from high school, even though you might have just worked with the same student as a high school senior! Suddenly it's the world of academia and experimentation and the avant-garde, of Beckett, Albee, and Stoppard, of naturalism versus realism, of eccentric professors and over-the-top designers, of thesis papers, of alternative theater spaces, and of outrageous acting exercises.

In my experience directing on a college level, the more "creative" you are the happier the students and faculty are going to be. It is an opportunity for a director to explore and embellish his or her own methods, to take risks that he or she wouldn't take in other venues. And for the most part, it seems that the actors in college productions not only accept a director who has alternative methods but welcome it. I'm not suggesting that you should play-act at being an eccentric, off-the-wall parody of what we've come to expect of an "acting teacher" in Greenwich Village. But if you lean in that direction, you wouldn't be out of place in many college theater programs.

Nontraditional casting, while good on any level of theater, is particularly welcome in a college setting. While on a high school level I interpreted nontraditional casting as primarily changing genders, the more universal definition would be to encourage the casting of ethnic and disabled actors in roles traditionally given to Caucasians. You might also find that your cast consists of a mixture of college students and outside talent. This will depend on the size and policy of the theater department, and on the student body. If you do cast outside the student body, it might color somewhat your approach to the show. Here is the opportunity to let your imagination run wild—to set *Company* in a subway if you'd like. It will be accepted far more readily than trying it at your local community theater or regional company.

As far as directing the actors you have finally cast, the same tasteful rules apply—nurturing and teaching plus patience and compassion—but you can deal with these actors on a more adult level than you might high school students. You can, and should, expect more of them because chances are they are serious about their craft and trying to earn a degree it in. You can expect them to come to the rehearsals more prepared. You should expect them to do extensive homework—and by this I mean to come to each rehearsal having worked at home (or in their dorm) on what was accomplished at the prior rehearsal. You can also expect them to have done homework by researching the play and their characters much they way you have as a director. Since ostensibly they are living and breathing theater on a "24/7" basis, you can demand a lot more preparation of them outside of the formal rehearsals.

During the first few rehearsals, go ahead and give out a few creative assignments. Have the cast create a back story for their characters. Ask them to research the time period, perhaps giving each of them a specific area to research such as clothing, living conditions, political climate, class structure—anything that can provide insight into the time period of the show. This sort of approach is perfect for the collegiate environment.

College actors should be at the peak of their cognitive skills. While I am not suggesting you come to a rehearsal unprepared—far from it—you can certainly enjoy more freedom to change and experiment and still have the actors stay with you and not get overly confused. My preferred directorial approach regardless of the situation is to get the show up on its feet in a rough form as early as possible, and then take a look at what I have. I can mold and enhance what I *see* much more easily than what I *read*, so seeing the actors walk through a scene is much more likely to spur my creative juices than when I first read the scene or hear it read aloud. This is particularly appropriate on a college level since the actors are game to try new ideas and to do variations on your themes.

College actors might also be very much in favor of developing a rapport with the director because they are hungry to learn as much as they can about their craft from as many people as possible. In their eyes, you have been brought in as a working professional, and as such you have technique and knowledge to share with them. And, of course, we hope this is indeed true! Treat them as collaborators. Let them bring to the table their ideas and impressions. If you explain early on that you are completely open to their input as long as they appreciate that you will make the final ruling, you may very well find alternative approaches to the material. Stay open to change. And encourage, even when you ultimately disagree with an idea.

The college experience can be a place for you as a director to grow, experiment, and explore more than any other venue. High school actors might not be ready for anything other than strong and decisive leadership; community theater performers may be too diverse in their backgrounds and too much might be riding financially on a regional theater project for this sort of freedom. Seize the opportunity if you get a chance to work at the college level.

Community Theater

My guess is that the great majority of the readers of this primer will find themselves working more often than not at some sort of community theater. Since the actors volunteering to work at community theaters will run the gamut from high school and college students and hobbyists to those with professional aspirations and moonlighting professionals, it is not terribly easy to define a directorial style for community theaters. You will have to adapt your style not only to the theater and the specific show you are working on, but often to individual actors as well.

What makes a good director of community theater? Certainly the same qualities that make for a good director of students—sensitivity, compassion, and the willingness to teach. But you have to add to the mix the ability to relate to the performers as their peer and their contemporary. Students in both the high school and college environments expect you to be older than they are and want to look up to you as an adult and a teacher. In community theater there will be people younger than you, of course, but also actors your own age and probably several who are quite older. You'll have to gain their respect no matter what the age difference right off the bat. You might have to overcome the wariness or resentment of some who look at you as an interloper or an upstart. There will be others who seem to "challenge" you to be good. You'll have to gain their confidence and respect, too, and the sooner you can do that, the better.

Despite my feelings that an initial read-through on the first day might be an unnecessary step in the rehearsal process, if this is your first directing assignment at an established community theater populated with many long-standing members, it might be a good idea. At this initial meeting you can hit the ground running, immediately involving the cast in your ideas for the show and your exciting directorial methods. If you are enthused, your enthusiasm will, with luck, rub off.

Based solely on my experience directing at many community theaters, here is a list of the types of actors you might encounter, and some tips on getting along well with them. This is based on the assumption that you have cast the show age appropriate. As an example, if you were doing *Oliver!* the workhouse kids would be preteens; Fagin's gang boys would be late teens; Nancy and Bill Sykes would be late twenties, early thirties; and Fagin and the other adults would be in their forties to sixties, or even older.

Preteens

There are two things to consider with the children in a community theater show. First and foremost, try to work with the children in the early part of the evening and not to keep them too late until you are actually in run-throughs. Depending on the kids themselves, as well as on how many of them are in your show, you might need what we affectionately call a "kid wrangler." This can be a volunteer adult or perhaps the parents of the children, set up on a rotating schedule. The kids can be entertained in the green room or the costume shop or wherever is convenient, and supplied with a TV and some tapes, puzzles, or other entertainment. The kid wrangler also makes sure every one of them makes his or her entrance on time, and in their proper costume.

While I am on the subject of parents, I don't wish to disparage them—many can be helpful, supportive, and concerned. But occasionally you'll come across a true stage mother or father, and if you do, you need to handle them with the proverbial kid gloves. If you find that they resist everything, from their child's costume to the rehearsal schedule, you may have to gently talk to them. Or post a sign: MAMA ROSE IS NOT ALLOWED BACKSTAGE AT THIS THEATER.

The second point to consider with children is how to actually direct them. You might find that they take direction well and can be talked to like any other actor. But sometimes you have to be more like their homeroom teacher, devising simple methods like hand gestures to keep them quiet, get them moving, and remind them to focus. Time outs are acceptable as well.

It is best to work slowly, in small chunks, and to review as often as possible—the method that works with most age groups! But what is also helpful is to find someone—an assistant, a willing cast member, or even a parent—who will review with the kids in another space every night they are called to rehearsal. They need to know their parts by rote, backward and forward, able to perform them even in their sleep. The slightest distraction can often throw a youngster, so the better they know the material, the safer you are.

Teenagers

You can pretty much adapt the methods described under working at a high school to teenagers, with two exceptions. The first is that they are no longer in their high school environment. This can work for or against you. Some teens may feel a certain freedom in an out-of-school rehearsal situation and test the waters. Others may react in the opposite manner, appreciating and respecting the responsibility that comes with being cast in a show outside of their school. Be prepared for both possibilities. Second—and this should definitely work in your favor—there is a good chance that being in the company of adult, and presumably more serious, actors will have a positive affect on the teens, elevating them to do their finest, and be on their best behavior.

Basically, if you treat the teens as adults, they will more often than not rise to the occasion and behave as such. One added benefit—you can sometimes utilize one of the teens to demonstrate a particularly exuberant piece of movement or choreography—they are, after all, probably more limber than you!

Young Adults

I'm referring here to actors from about twenty years of age through their fifties. Here is where you'll find your most eclectic group of performers. There will be the hardcore community theater performers who love to be in shows; the "newbies," who are just exploring the art of local theater; and those who are perhaps looking at your show as an opportunity for socializing. Within each of these categories you will have varying degrees of talent—from those who are really ready to do this professionally to those who need to be taught basic Acting 101 more than they need direction.

This group of performers will test your people skills more than any other, and since you need to deal differently with virtually each of the performers and their specific traits, you will be constantly adapting and morphing throughout each rehearsal. The ones who have their craft more or less mastered will expect you to cater to them. They'll want character analysis and motivation as soon as they know their blocking—sometimes even before! During notes, they might be restless when notes are for others since they feel that everyone should be coming along at their pace.

While some may not have much patience for those performers who are not quite at their level, others will be quick to volunteer to coach their fellow actors. This may not be exactly what you want. This can also happen with an actor who has previously directed—some of them can divorce themselves from codirecting while others just can't help offering advice, corrections, and other directorial tidbits. You'll need to gently explain to those actors who are either impatient or overly helpful that they need to let everyone work and grow at their own pace. This is actually something a director needs to keep in mind as well. Every actor works at his or her own pace.

Some will struggle right up until tech week. They may have trouble remembering the lines or certain parts of the blocking or choreography. They might not master the accent or speech patterns and rhythms. These performers will need special hand-holding and encouragement. While the temptation might be to get frustrated with them, showing that frustration can do more harm than good.

They know they're behind (at least you hope they know) and the best approach is to ask them how you can best help. Would they like some private coaching? Does some part of the blocking not feel right to them—would some adjustments help? Compassion is the key—even when you might prefer to throw up your hands.

Then there will be those actors who nail everything early on in the rehearsal process. This might seem like a wonderful thing, but it is a mixed blessing. There is a tendency for this type of actor to get bored once they feel they mastered what has been given them, and for them to then try alternative choices to moments or entire scenes. Unfortunately, these alternatives are not always improvements, and so you must explain that the actor needs to trust what works and just go with it. Allow the actor to occasionally pull back a bit and not work at performance level—that simple variation can help with boredom sometimes, as well as give the actor a sense that you appreciate just how professional he is by allowing him to not give his all at every rehearsal!

Between these two extremes are those actors who seem to time their growth with your rehearsal schedule. They come to each successive rehearsal having worked on what was given to them, ready to absorb at the pace you've set. This doesn't make them any better or worse that anyone else, but it is nice to work with someone who seems to neither rush nor lag behind your guidance.

Actors need to feel that they are the center of your attention. It is a trick you must learn to make them feel that they have your undivided attention even though your mind is not only on them but on everything else as well. You'll often be approached by an actor who asks, "Did you see that moment when I . . . ?" or "Was that okay when I . . . ?" While lying isn't the answer, if you didn't happen to notice the perhaps subtle embellishment, you can still be encouraging by saying that you hadn't caught it but would make sure you paid special attention the next time the scene is run. Then make sure you do so!

Part of the key to being a successful director is the ability to visualize what I affectionately think of as *the big picture*. The actors can only see what is happening in their little world—how they are delivering their lines or how they are interacting with fellow actors. To them, the scene went well if everyone remembered their lines and blocking, and perhaps there was even some chemistry between the performers. But the director feels the scene went well only when the actors did their job *and* the set shifted smoothly and on time, *and* the costumes were being worn properly and complemented each other, *and* the telephone sound effect went off on cue, *and* lights went on when the light switch was flipped, *and* . . . well, you get the idea.

This chapter is about directing actors, and I don't mean to deviate too far from its purpose, but how the actors play a scene is interdependent on everything else that happens in the scene—the sets, the lights, the props, the costumes, and the sounds. Always keep *the big picture* foremost in your mind.

As far as the actors who are there primarily to socialize are concerned, the best tack you can take is to try to inspire them to "get into" the theatrical experience as much as possible. This will not negate their socializing, especially anything they might do after the rehearsals or on breaks—and it just might give them two reasons to have a great time—the theater aspect and the socializing.

Elder Actors

There is nothing more effective than casting an actor of the proper age to play a grandfather or elder statesman or an old-age pensioner. While a good actor with proper makeup can certainly play older than his years, the audience is usually aware that they are watching a younger actor in the role. But older actors bring their own set of unique challenges. I have found you need to handle elderly actors in a manner similar to the very young—art imitates life yet again.

Going slow and constant repetition are good methods, but unlike youngsters, the seniors are liable to be impatient with their own inability to remember things as well as they used to. They tend to feel uncomfortable with certain bits of blocking or choreography simply because they cannot do what they used to be able to do. You may have to adapt your original ideas to fit their limitations.

Equity Theater

There are certain assumptions you can make when you are hired to direct an Equity show: Since you are paying half or more of the actors, you can assume you will not have to settle when casting the production. You can also presuppose that the actors you do cast will have had sufficient training and experience that you won't be giving acting lessons. You can expect them to have the discipline and the training to know what is expected at rehearsals; to have their lines memorized in a timely fashion, and to adjust to your directorial changes accordingly.

But you know what they say about assumptions! Depending on your geographic location, you might not have an abundance of Equity performers to choose from, and you can never predict anyone's abilities until you've worked with them.

When planning rehearsals for an Equity show, you will need to work in tandem with your Equity stage manager. There are very specific rules about how many rehearsals you can hold within a given week, how long and how often the actors should be given breaks, and so forth. In fact, there are Equity rules governing almost everything, from how much crossover space there is behind the scenery to the rake of a platform. But at the heart of it, you are still working with actors, and the same rules of compassion and understanding, of course, apply.

What changes is the speed at which you work. Rather than sporadic rehearsals over six or seven weeks, most likely you are working regular eight-hour days for two or three weeks. When you see everyone day after day in a regimented schedule, you can set up rehearsals in a more compact fashion.

I still believe that getting the show blocked and into run-throughs as soon as possible is the best way to see if things are working or not. If you are working on a nonmusical and have two weeks, blocking the show in the first two to three days might be in order. As long as the cast is not overloaded and seem to retain everything, keep moving forward at a brisk pace. Many actors can remember their lines best when they relate them to a bit of blocking or stage business, so having the show on its feet early will also help with memorization. The sooner the actors are off book, the sooner you can start to truly pull scenes apart for pacing, laughs, or dramatic tension. You can then get down to what the actors really want to do—act.

If you have the framework of entrances, exits, crosses, and stage business prepared beforehand and if you teach it to your cast in a short period of time, the rest of the rehearsal can be spent exploring, experimenting and, as they say in theater vernacular, cementing (coming up with a finished product). You are then allowed a number of 10-out-of-12-hour rehearsals, which means you can rehearse for 10 hours on one or two days. These are usually your tech rehearsals.

This is the time to guide your actors through movement on the set as well as the use of the properties and costumes. A musical is more difficult simply because of the added elements of song and dance. After a week or two in an empty hall, the addition of tech elements can be daunting. If you understand that, you can be reassuring and comforting rather than short-tempered.

In an Equity situation, the use of time is crucial, and so professional rehearsals often split up until run-throughs are established. It is not uncommon for the choreographer to be working with the ensemble while the director is working on scenes with principals in a separate space and the musical director teaches music to another splinter group. This takes much preproduction planning, not only to coordinate the rehearsals but also to ensure that the creative team is on the same page. An entire week may go by before everyone sees how all the pieces are fitting together.

Equity actors are professionals, so you'll want to treat them as such. If, however, you find this not to be true with a particular actor, it is not quite as simple a task to make your unhappiness known as it might be in an amateur situation. While you certainly would gently and respectfully discuss the issues first, serious disciplinary action would most likely go through the Equity stage manager in accordance with current Equity guidelines.

Final Thoughts

Every director is different and will approach the rehearsal period in their own way, based on their circumstances, training, and experience. But certain basic rules of thumb emerge regardless of the level of theater in which you are working. Actors, in a sense, are like children. They need the discipline of a strong director and work best when clear expectations are established, but they also need a certain amount of freedom to learn and to grow. And like a parent–child relationship, kindness and love go a lot further than anger and sarcasm. The actors tend to become a temporary but close-knit family during rehearsals, and the creative staff become surrogate parents. And as with any family, there will be ups and downs. Embrace this volatility and make it work for you. To borrow from a song by Stephen Sondheim: "Actors may not obey, but actors will listen. Careful the words you say, actors will hear, and learn."

11

Miscellaneous

This chapter is more or less a catchall for random thoughts, advice, anecdotes, and tidbits. Herewith are directorial issues that didn't quite fall under the other topics.

The Play's the Thing

It is infinitely better to make changes that allow the actor to be seen in the best possible light than to settle for a less-than-perfect performance simply because you are holding on to your original concepts. A director must always remember that the audience isn't aware of what it took to get to the actual performances; they only see what is in front of them. I have had many a director say to me: "Well, I know this isn't great, but you should have seen it three weeks ago."

Whether the admission charge is $65 a ticket or free, the director has an obligation to the audience to convey the playwright's purpose. This might be to enlighten, to educate, to move the audience, or purely to entertain them. As is often quoted, "the play's the thing," and the audience should not be distracted from the play itself by technical issues or poor performances. So a director and his team should never settle. Any problem can be resolved or masked in some way with proper thought and consideration.

Not every actor is a triple threat. Inexperienced performers can be stiff or deliver stilted line readings. They might not seem natural or comfortable. It is the director's challenge to minimize the actor's flaws and accentuate the positive! If the actor can't hold a harmony, then ultimately you have to settle on melody. Better that than sour notes. If the actor has trouble with a line delivery, than you must take him aside and privately coach him (or her). There have been instances where I have delivered lines into a cassette recorder for an actor to keep playing until they could mimic me. Is this ideal? Of course not. Can it be somewhat degrading or embarrassing to the performer? Possibly. But ultimately, what occurs in front of the audience is what is important, and better to have an uncomfortable moment at a rehearsal than a poor performance.

People's egos can be wounded and feelings hurt among the design staff as well, but as long as you are polite and compassionate, you are within your right to request a change to a costume that isn't appropriate or a set piece that isn't working. Even though the designers attend rehearsals and watch run-throughs, it is frequently impossible to know how well their designs will be integrated until tech week. Suddenly a dancer cannot execute a dance step in the dress, or a piece of scenery is too tall and keeps knocking a light out of focus. Something has to give: do you change the dance step or the costume; do you cut down the scenery or move the light?

This sort of resolution becomes the director's decision—and it is not a matter of pointing fingers or who is to blame. Problems of this sort are quite normal in theater, and the director needs to be able to think on his feet and come up with the best solution for the show. Someone is going to be disappointed, someone's work is going to be compromised, and so the director needs to be a diplomat. But the integrity of the show is the bottom line. It's all part of directing.

Using the Space

With the subheading "Using the Space" I am actually referring to two separate considerations. The first is utilizing the physical design of the type of theater you are working in to plan the overall concept for your production, and the second is using the theater space to its best advantage when staging your show.

Using the theater's physical design is a bit obvious. If you are in a one-hundred-seat black-box space with a tiny stage, it will, to some degree, dictate the type of show that can be done successfully. It would be inappropriate to try and stage *Noises Off* in such a theater, what with its two-story set design, usually placed on a revolve. Act 1 of *Noises Off* is a country house with two levels and tons of doors, all of which need escapes on the upstage side. Then the whole set revolves for act 2 and we see all the scaffolding and platforms and escapes of the set. There just would not be enough room to build and house the structure of the set. On the other hand, a small three-character show such as *American Buffalo* might fit perfectly, even though it also has a realistic set. *Buffalo* takes place in a cramped junk shop, so the small space would work for you.

These concerns may fall to a producer, but often theaters turn to their directors to suggest plays, especially if the director has a good track record. Choosing the right show for the space will go a long way to its successful mounting.

Regarding the second use of space, experience has proven that certain areas of a stage have more "weight" or importance than others. Traditionally the stage is broken up into six quadrants—downstage center (DSC), downstage left and downstage right, upstage center and upstage left and right. Some directors break it down further, with ten quadrants in two horizontal lines that include downstage and upstage far right and left, or nine quadrants that have a downstage center, midstage center and upstage center with its respective lefts and rights. Regardless, downstage is a more powerful staging position than upstage, and downstage center is the most weighty or important spot on the stage. It should be used judiciously, as it telegraphs to an audience that whoever occupies this primary spot of real estate is quite important indeed. Mama Rose would finish "Rose's Turn" DSC at the end of *Gypsy*.

An actor entering upstage and crossing downstage has more psychological impact than merely entering laterally from a down-stage wing. Stage right holds more "power" than stage left. I doubt this is a political statement. Maybe it is because we read from left to right. Keeping these tricks in mind while planning your blocking will give your staging a subtle but dramatic impact.

Levels also have their effect. An actor standing on a chair or a garden wall or a few steps up a staircase will be more commanding than those on stage level. An abstract set with assorted levels of varying heights presents infinitely more staging possibilities than a flat stage.

Stage Pictures

I am a firm believer that creating memorable stage pictures is one of the director's and choreographer's duties. Whenever there are more than a handful of actors on stage, a director should be cognizant of their spatial relationships and what each actor is doing, whether standing or sitting and observing. I often tell a cast that any actor who sets foot on the stage must be "alive" and "in the moment" regardless of the size of the role. If an audience's attention drifts from the main characters and turns to an ensemble or supporting cast member, they should witness a totally entertaining show unto itself.

I like to look at a scene as if I am taking photos. Regardless of where I point my lens, I should be presented with a beautifully positioned photo opportunity. I once worked on a very interesting, tiny musical by the authors of *The Fantasticks* called *Philemon*. Much of the show takes place in a damp and dismal dungeon and the ensemble huddles crouched in various corners of the set, scared, hungry, and miserable. We worked extensively on their body language and heartbreaking facial expressions. The entire message of the show was apparent in each one of these prisoners at any point in the evening. I worked equally hard on *Marat/Sade*, a show in which the inmates of an asylum rarely leave the stage. What an opportunity for an ensemble member to shine!

When creating a musical, your use of the ensemble (a much-preferred term to "chorus") to create stage pictures is quite important, and the possibilities are great. Left to their own devices, principal actors will tend to stand in a straight line when five or more of them are in a scene. Add in the ensemble, and you have the chorus line syndrome—any moment you expect them to break into "I really need this job." In real life, however, we don't form a line when we gather together, we *group*. By having some of the actors stand a bit upstage and by having others form little triangular groups, you can change a stilted and boring image into a picture that is both alive and interesting.

If your stage set has levels, use them. This will also help to break up a stagnant picture and make it more visually appealing. Consider levels of all types—not only levels of varying heights but levels of depth, downstage to upstage. Unless you really are trying for a chorus line effect, or staging curtain calls, stay away from a line that is parallel to your apron. Diagonals, triangles, semicircles and "clumps" are much preferable—in staging and in choreography. And as obvious as this may sound, always keep in mind that principals are best positioned downstage when sharing a scene with the ensemble.

Last, it is important to make sure the audience's attention focuses where you want it to; to help this, appropriate gestures are sometimes necessary. As an example, take the song "Wells Fargo Wagon" from *The Music Man*. In this production number, many of the ensemble members have solos. Without a raised hand or a step forward, it is often difficult to discern just where the voices are coming from. This problem is compounded when everyone is miked into a monophonic sound system—all the voices come from the same speakers.

Line Readings

It can confuse an audience when an actor delivers his line with the emphasis on the wrong word. In extreme cases it can actually distort the author's meaning; at a minimum it will merely sound odd. When this happens, try to correct the error—by example if need be—so that the actor doesn't learn it incorrectly and have trouble relearning it.

Here's a fictitious example: "I went to the store." Is it a sentence about already having been to the store? I *went* to the store. Is it about who went to the store? *I* went to the store. Or is it about where you went? I went to the *store*. With the incorrect emphasis, the sentence is stilted, and the meaning isn't clear.

Ch-Ch-Ch-Changes

On Broadway there is a point at which the show is "frozen," meaning it is no longer going to be changed. Once a show opens on Broadway, after the series of preview performances, the director's job is finished and the stage manager takes over, making sure the production remains genuine and fresh. While this holds true for most Equity regional productions as well, I don't believe that an amateur show need be frozen; I have made changes right up until the final performance. It all depends on whether or not you are going to continue to attend performances and tweak the show once it opens.

Something very interesting happens when you suddenly play the show in front of an audience. There are laughs where you didn't expect them. You get a feel for what makes the audience restless, and what makes them sit in rapt attention. You can begin to watch the show for content and clarity, rather than worrying if the set is going to come on properly or if an actor knows his lines. Chances are you'll see moments that you missed in the madness of tech, or because you were sitting too close to the stage while directing. It would be a shame not to correct or enhance these moments.

In my opinion the only difference now is the manner in which you give the notes. Whereas during the rehearsal period you would assemble the cast after a rehearsal, it is now probably unfair to keep the cast after a show—they have friends in the audience plus they should go home and get some rest. The best way to tweak the show once it is up and running is to call the cast together before "half-hour"—the time they use for makeup and getting ready, and before the audience is let into the theater.

If the changes are minor, you can just explain them—but if they involve a number of people you would want to run it quickly on stage. In every case, make sure everyone knows of the change—from all those on stage to those running the sound and lights to the stage manager—if not, cues might be called wrong or other actors' performances might be thrown off.

It might be helpful to alert the cast and crew to changes via email before the next performance—this will give the actors and staff a chance to think about them, digest them, and come prepared to work through them. Not everyone can adjust to change easily, and the more preparation and time you can give them, the more successful they will be. But never be hesitant to improve the production. Both the audience's reaction and your own distance from the rehearsal process can provide new insight into the show.

Pep Talks

Throughout the rehearsals, your notes are most likely to be constructive criticism rather than praise. Therefore it is beneficial to occasionally give a pep talk to the cast to let them know that everything is on track. This might be done as general praise to the entire company at the end of a note session, or by letting each of the actors know what they are doing right before you proceed with notes.

If rehearsals run late and notes run even longer, a positive email to the cast the next day emphasizing how all their hard work is paying off can give them a boost that will confidently affect the next rehearsal. You should be encouraging at least every few rehearsals.

The night before tech week is a definite time to give a pep talk, letting them know that they are in good enough shape to face the ardors of the coming week. This is the time to highlight everything that is good about the production thus far, for surely there will be plenty of room for improvement once you add in all the technical elements.

Since everyone benefits from praise and encouragement, the next mandatory time for a pep talk would be after dress rehearsal or right before opening night. Like a coach sending the team out to win the big game, you need to psych the actors into doing their best on opening—a time fraught with nerves.

Many casts like to give a group hug or hold hands in a circle or perform some other ritual before each show—why not let them? I have no idea how or where it started, but I'll send each cast out every night by encouraging them to "kick ass [or kick butt if there are kids in the cast] out there." They've come to expect it and, since theater is full of superstitions, I do it every night. I save "break a leg" for my opening night cards to the actors.

One more mandatory pep talk: before the *second* performance. Time and time again it is the second night that has the most flubs and mishaps, and the reason is simple—the second night can be a let-down from opening. The actors need to be made aware through the director (or stage manager) that since they are no longer running on adrenaline and sheer excitement they must be on their toes, using their brains rather than their hearts to power the second performance. They must never let down their guard and must be constantly thinking so that the audience sees the best possible show. I guess I'm superstitious as well; invariably the performance falls apart whenever I skip a second night pep talk!

Curtain Calls

Curtain calls can range from the most simple to quite complicated (consider the "megamix" at the end of *Joseph and the Amazing Technicolor Dreamcoat*—a fifteen-minute curtain call!). What is important is that the curtain call be appropriate. At the end of a three-character drama, having the principals simply walk downstage and bow in unison once or twice might be perfectly in keeping with the mood of the play. On the other hand, an elaborate call that involves dance and song might be the perfect ending on a big musical.

If it is in keeping with the style of the show, it is often fun to have the actors begin their curtain calls in character, then "break character" to bow. Or, little bits of stage business that are reminiscent of staging seen during the play can be repeated at the curtain call. A young actor playing an old person might remove her wig in front of the audience at their bow, or a performer who plays several roles might take his bow wearing bits of both costumes.

The order of the curtain calls is dictated by the size of the roles. For a nonmusical, you have to decide whether the show is an ensemble-style show, without clearly defined leading roles, or whether there are definite supporting character parts and major leads. For a true ensemble show such as *Art*, where there are three equal characters, you might choose to have all three actors come out together. Even if they then take an individual bow, the fact that they came out for the curtain call together denotes equal roles.

In a play such as *The Royal Family*, where there are small roles, bit players, and large leading roles, you'd have the small roles come out first, often grouped together in pairs or even trios and quartets. As the roles get larger, you can still have duos bow together, especially if they play husband and wife or two villains, leading eventually to solo bows for your stars. If a man and woman come out together, the man usually bows first and then gestures to the woman to bow or curtsey. You can add interest to the bows by having each character retire somewhere on the set, forming an interesting picture, and then rejoin the line for the company bow.

In a musical, it tends to start with the ensemble. Any memorable cameo roles or featured dancers would be next, perhaps stepping forward out of the line. The ensemble would then step back and part, leaving a center aisle, (or some interesting variation on this theme) to allow the supporting cast to come through to center. With musicals, the "bow music" often suggests entrances. If cleverly written, musical themes change to highlight certain characters. Generally, after the final "star" bow there would be a company bow, an acknowledgment by the cast to the orchestra, another company bow, and then actors would "peel" off in the opposite order they came on, leaving the lead(s) for a final bow as the curtain comes down.

A word of advice. Don't leave the bows until the last minute. It is the last image an audience sees, and you want it to be as powerful as the show. Curtain calls take rehearsal. Plan them early in tech week.

12

A Little Help from My Friends

As producing director of Plays-in-the-Park, I am surrounded daily by theater people—other directors, designers, artisans, and plenty of actors. I thought it might be a fitting close for this book to reach out to a cross section of them and see what they thought it takes to make a good director. I was hoping it would prove both fun and constructive, and it did.

I sent an email off to various colleagues and asked two simple questions:

1. What makes a good director good?
2. What does it take to be a really good director?

Similar questions, but with a subtle difference. I wanted to address the intangibles that separate an average director from a great one.

The responses were very interesting and, as I predicted, were colored by which side of the curtain the person responding worked on. The directors approached the questions with a slant that varied from the designers, and both varied dramatically from the actor's point of view. A number of the replies came from theater people who worked in the academic world, and their answers were quite different from those of people who freelanced for various theaters.

Several themes emerged:

- A love of theater is paramount. A director must love every moment spent on the script and rehearsal.
- The director should have considerable knowledge in all areas of theater. They felt that the best shows are the ones

that look as if one person created the entire production. A good director will understand both the value and impact of every theatrical element including lighting, sets, props, music, dance, sound, and costumes.

- Almost everyone echoed my motto: paying attention to details—no matter how minor—is what separates the pros from the amateurs.
- A director must have a basic respect for all that he or she works with, and be the consummate professional.
- Among the actors, the great majority felt that a good director was one who both guides the actor as to what to do while leaving plenty of room for the actor to discover and experiment.

There were also a large number of original and perceptive thoughts that stood out, which I have paraphrased and embellished as well.

- A director needs to be able to visualize, imagine, and hear every moment in the entire production. This includes every entrance and exit, scene shift, light cue, and line of dialogue.
- A director needs to have the skills that allow him or her to communicate every vision to both the production team and the company.
- A director knows when to accept suggestions and when to reject them.
- It takes nerve, cunning, guile, wit, strength, patience, and power to be a great director.
- A director needs organizational skills and a clear but always flexible strategy.
- A director must be able to multitask.
- A director understands and can work within budgets, limitations, and deadlines.
- A director needs to be the leader but also needs to work well with the team, allowing them to execute their jobs artistically while giving them guidance and insight into the overall vision of the show.

- One of the responses was from an actress—a very good one I might add—who wrote: "A good director is someone who has read the play and actually knows what is going on!" While this may seem like a gag, she was perfectly serious, and it exemplifies the evidence of the lack of training and experience sometimes found in high schools and community theater directors who may think, "How hard can it be? I've been in a show before!"

To sum up, I would like to paraphrase a definition I heard attributed to a famous professional director:

You have to be able to answer hundreds of questions every day, from the length of a hem to the color of a light, from an inflection of a line delivery to the tempo of a piece of music. And if you don't know the answer, you need to be able to make it up!

Final Thoughts

Not everyone can be a great director. There are qualities a great director needs that most likely cannot be learned by reading a book or taking a class. The innate sense of leadership, the artistic talent, and the people skills are traits that might be more a product of DNA than classrooms. But if the raw material is there, you can indeed embellish, enhance, and perfect your craft, and a good director can become great. Perhaps experience is the key, especially if you learn and grow from each time up at bat.

If you want to be a director, and you feel you are or can be good at it, then go out there and work—and keep working until you are great, and then keeping working long after that. Start off small, and work your way up. Experiment. Take chances.

And pay attention to the details.